Contents

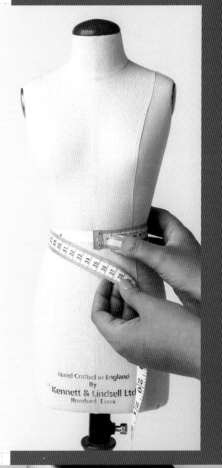

INTRODUCTION

Being self-taught, making clothes from scratch with just a few basic body measurements has always been a passion of mine. And as my sewing journey progresses and I continue to explore this way of making clothes, this time I wanted to focus on one specific garment: the skirt.

Just like the #sewingrevolution, *Your Skirt, Your Way* is designed to empower you to get sewing with just a few body measurements, creating clothes that reflect your personality and transform how you look and feel. Here, I will show you how to draft a block (or sloper if you're in the US) for your unique body, then adapt it to design and create the perfect skirt for any occasion. This book will take you through drafting and creating your made-to-measure basic skirt block (pages 22–37); show you how to cut and splice your block to create different skirt shapes (pages 38–51); then how to add your choice of fastenings, from waistbands to fly zip fronts (pages 52–65). To finish, you will add those special individual details like pockets and yokes (pages 66–83) to create your perfect skirt.

I like to think of this book as giving you the ingredients to make skirt recipes, so even though I take you through ten different skirt designs (pages 88–127), *Your Skirt, Your Way* will be your 'cookbook' for so many other recipes!

I can't wait to see what you sew up, so don't forget to share pictures of your makes: use #sewingrevolution. ENJOY!
Find me on Facebook: Tailor-Taylor

Follow @jennibobtaylor on Twitter and Instagram
Visit my website: www.jenniffertaylor.co.uk
#sewingrevolution

YOUR SKIRT,
Your Way

> DRAFT YOUR BLOCK,
> CHOOSE YOUR SHAPE,
> CUSTOMIZE YOUR OWN DESIGN!

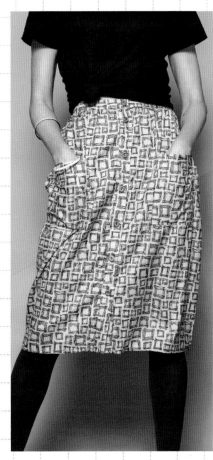

JENNIFFER TAYLOR

SEARCH PRESS

First published in 2021

Search Press Limited
Wellwood, North Farm Road, Tunbridge Wells,
Kent TN2 3DR

Text copyright © Jenniffer Taylor 2021

Photographs by Mark Davison: 2, 4, 5t, 6, 7, 8, 13, 14,
15, 16–17, 19, 20bl, 22, 24–25, 29, 31, 32, 33, 34, 35, 36,
37, 38, 39, 40, 41, 42, 43, 44, 45, 46, 47, 48, 49, 50, 51,
54, 55, 56, 57, 58, 59, 60, 61, 62, 63, 64, 65, 68, 69,
70, 71tl, 71tr, 72, 73, 74, 75, 76, 78, 79, 80, 81, 82, 88,
92, 96, 100, 104, 108, 112, 116, 120, 124.
Photographs by Stacy Grant: 1, 3, 5b, 9, 10, 11, 52, 53,
66, 67, 71b, 77, 83, 84–85, 86, 87, 89, 90, 91, 93, 94,
95, 97, 98, 99, 101, 102, 103, 105, 106, 107, 109, 110, 111,
113, 114, 115, 117, 118, 119, 121, 122, 123, 125, 126, 127, 128.
Photographs by Roddy Paine: 20br, 21, 26, 27.

Photographs and design copyright ©
Search Press Ltd 2021

All the step-by-step photographs in this book
feature the author, Jenniffer Taylor.

ISBN: 978-1-78221-593-6

The projects in this book have been made using
metric measurements, and the imperial equivalents
provided have been calculated following standard
conversion practices. The imperial measurements
are often rounded to the nearest ⅛in for ease of
use. If you need more exact measurements, there
are a number of excellent online converters that
you can use. Always use either metric or imperial
measurements, not a combination of both.

For details of suppliers, please visit the
Search Press website: www.searchpress.com

Visit Jenniffer's website:
www.jennifertaylor.co.uk
Search for Tailor-Taylor on Facebook
Follow @JenniBobTaylor on Twitter

Acknowledgements

To Ayia's amazing Nannies – Lain and Brenda; completing this book
would not have been possible without your caring hands and hearts
as you supported me and looked after our little squirrel.

To Sally: thank you for being my sounding board, for encouraging
me with my crazy ideas and plans and, most of all, for drinking red
wine with me and being a rock in my crazy world!

A huge thank you to Korbond and Vlieseline for your continued
support with the #sewingrevolution. To Kennett & Lindsell Ltd. for
letting me borrow the beautiful mannequins and to Janome for
supplying me with a new workhorse.

To the Search Press team and my wonderful editor and fellow
new mommy, Becky Robbins! Thank you for all your support and
patience. After two pregnancies (Imogen – Becky's beautiful little
girl – and Ayia), maternity leaves and postponed deadlines while I
got to grips with being a new mom to a daughter who doesn't like
to sleep, we finally got there! I'm so pleased we got to work together
again, and on this project, Becky.

Finally, to my two punks: my husband, Kirk, and little prayer,
Ayia Mala. What a rollercoaster three years! There is so much to say,
but most of all – you are my strength, the fire in my stomach, the
love in my heart.
Thank you for being my team.

HOW TO USE THIS BOOK

The reason I love making my own clothes is that it gives me the freedom to make garments that reflect my style, in my size. *Your Skirt, Your Way* gives you that same freedom: here you'll find all the 'ingredients' – the details, fixtures, features and shapes that you need to make your perfect skirt. By simply adding or removing different 'ingredients', you are creating different skirt 'recipes'... meaning that this easy-to-follow book actually gives you everything you need to create your ultimate skirt collection. And the beauty of it is – it all starts with a basic skirt block that is made to fit your unique size.

1 Firstly we are going to create the basic skirt block from which all your designs will originate. Using your measurements we are going to draft, toile and fit your unique and perfectly tailored skirt block (see pages 22–37) – sounds scary, but it really isn't!

2 Using this block we can start to create skirt 'recipes' – to do this you will need to consider three things:

• What overall shape do I want?
  Imagine the silhouette of your skirt: do you want it to be flared or A-line; short or long? With many different options to choose from, you will learn how to cut, splice and pivot your basic skirt block to create the shape(s) you want (see pages 38–51).

• How am I going to get in and out of my skirt?
  Decide whether you fancy a waistband or facing, a zip or buttons. You will learn how to adapt your block and create patterns to add these elements on pages 52–65.

• What extra details do I want to add?
  Do you want pockets, a yoke or a fancy hemline finish? Learn how to adapt your block and add detail to your skirt on pages 66–82.

3 Then all that's left to do is put your skirt together. When I first think about creating a skirt, I like to use my mini mannequin as a way of playing around with design ideas and working out construction riddles before committing to my full-size version, and that's what you'll see thoughout most of the book. Things are much easier to see and understand when they are in miniature. But don't worry – all instructions are in real size, so they'll be easy to follow. With the 10 designs in this book, I have done all of the constuctional thinking for you – there are step-by-step instructions guiding you through each one. And as for giving other designs a go yourself, I have outlined a basic guide to skirt construction (see page 86), which will direct you as to when and how to add the 'ingredients' to create your skirt.

So now you have everything you need to cook up your own wonderful skirt recipes... Let's get making your skirt, your way!

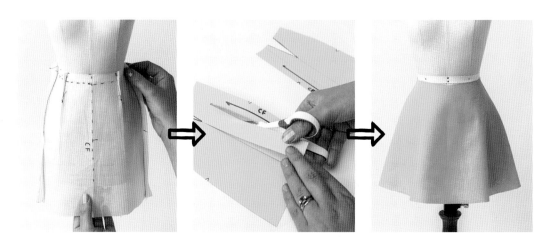

GETTING STARTED

BASIC SEWING KIT

Sharp things

Rule number one: padlock your dressmaking scissors and don't let anyone else use them! Rule number two: don't use your fabric scissors for anything else other than fabric! This may sound a little crazy, but investing in a pair of fabric scissors and only using them on fabric makes all the difference! Cutting things like paper, sticky tape, food packets, flower stems and so on, will blunt them and then potentially ruin your fabric when cutting it. I like to have a separate pair for paper and then a pair of embroidery scissors for loose threads and smaller precision cuts.

Top tip

I put my embroidery scissors onto a piece of long ribbon and wear them like a necklace. It stops me from losing them when in full-on dressmaking mode and also I feel like a proper seamstress with a scissor necklace and my tape measure around my neck!

Pinking shears are very handy for quickly finishing off your seams. The saw-toothed edge helps to stop your fabrics from fraying as much as a normal straight cut would, meaning your makes will stand up to a lot more washing and wearing.

A seamstress's best friend is an unpicker or quick unpick. We all dream of sewing without making a mistake, but you WILL make mistakes. In fact, I encourage it! Making mistakes is the best way to learn and some of my 'mistakes' have turned out to be awesome in the end so don't be afraid to make them. But when you really do need to unpick, a sharp unpicker is a must. Change your unpicker as soon as you notice it becoming blunt, as you don't want to start damaging your fabric. A sharp unpicker should glide through a seam without much force.

Top tip

The red ball is like a safety ball – it should stop you from cutting the fabric as you cut the threads.

A rotary cutter is great if you are making your own bias binding or cutting slippery fabrics. A rotary cutter looks and works just like a pizza cutter, meaning you can cut your fabric while it is completely flat. When using scissors, you will end up lifting your fabric as the blades cut through it; when dealing with slippy fabrics like silk or chiffon, this cutting motion can sometimes cause cutting errors if the fabric moves around. Ultimately, this is not an essential tool, but it's something to add to your sewing kit as you get more experienced. You will need a cutting mat to go with it.

Pins and needles

You can pick up needles very easily – even in the supermarket – and they sometimes come in a variety pack or compact. These are perfect as they will include everything you need, from small sharp needles to a wool needle. If you struggle to thread a needle, I would suggest picking up a couple of needle threaders too.

When buying pins, I always go for glass-headed ones because they won't melt under a hot iron. I find professional dressmakers' pins (which are the metal ones with no head) really fiddly, but hey, it's a personal preference. When you get more adventurous with different types of fabrics, you may want to invest in some longer, thinner pins, but they're not essential.

A spare pack of sewing-machine needles is also good to have. There's nothing worse than having to stop and shop because you have broken a sewing-machine needle. They tend to come in a variety of sizes to cover lightweight to heavier fabrics and include stretch/ballpoint needles, which you will need for stretchy fabrics. With sewing-machine needles, the lower the number, the finer the needle – great for finer fabrics. The higher the number, the thicker the needle – ideal for thicker fabrics. Try to get into the habit of changing your sewing-machine needle after a few projects. Just like your unpicker, your needle will become blunt over time and will start to chew up your fabric. So always do a test sew on a scrap piece of fabric before your start on your project. It's better to be safe than sorry.

Whether handmade or purchased, a pincushion is a must for keeping those pins and needles in one place. If you are going to buy a pincushion, it might be worth investing in an emery pincushion – these keep your pins and needles nice and sharp. Keep an eye out for the tomato-shaped pincushion with a little chilli shape attached to it – the chilli part is filled with emery powder. Pass your needle through the chilli a few times and it will sharpen your needle for you, making it last longer – bonus!

Made to measure

The iconic measuring tape is a sewing-kit essential and was the start of my measuring-device obsession. We will be talking more about pattern masters and tailor's curves later (see pages 16–17), but I truly believe you can never have enough measuring devices. Whether it's your old-school rulers, hemming rulers or sewing gauges (or as I call them: thingamabobs!), they are all useful and can make your dressmaking and pattern drafting life a lot easier and quicker.

Making a mark

There are so many different ways to mark your fabric. I sometimes use a pin, and tailor's tacks (see page 33) are always useful, but at other times you need to add a little more information than just mark a point on the fabric. Tailor's chalk is the traditional way to mark your fabric and can be easily brushed away. Chalk wheels and chalk pens are the same material, just packaged differently. What you use will come down to personal preference.

Hot things

An iron and an ironing board are must-haves. The good news is that the one you use for your laundry is perfect. However, it's also good to have an ironing cloth, or something that withstands heat like a clean tea towel to hand; when using

delicate or manmade fibres and when fusing interfacing to your fabrics you don't want to melt your fabric or ruin your iron, so it's worth having a piece of cloth ready to place over the top to protect your fabric before you press.

Tailor's hams and sleeve boards are indispensable. Tailor's hams come in different shapes and sizes, and will help to create shape when pressing a garment. A sleeve board is basically a small ironing board that makes pressing sleeves and cuffs a lot easier. These tools can make the difference between a good finish and a professional finish, as well as just making the job a lot easier for you. Check out my tailor's ham tutorial online if you want to make one yourself.

The unusual suspects

A lint roller is not something you might automatically include in your sewing kit, but it has become my firm favourite for removing threads that have been unpicked from a toile or garment. Not forgetting that it's also the quickest way to tidy my sewing area!

Elastic is a must-have item even though, in this book, we won't be inserting it into any garments. The elastic will be your fitting buddy... (everything will be revealed later, when we take your body measurements, see pages 26–27).

Chopsticks are the perfect poking tool. You can buy point turners very cheaply, but as you will probably already have a chopstick in your kitchen, just grab that instead. A chopstick is awesome for poking out your corners or pushing out waistbands, as the slightly rounded edge stops you from punching a hole in your fabric.

Although you have your own body to work with, I find a dress form is a useful tool that allows me to easily play around with design ideas; a miniature dress form, as used throughout this book and shown right, is a fantastic tool for trying out design ideas and working out garment construction without having to use lots of fabric. You can buy mini dress forms like this one, which are scaled-down versions of the real thing. However, you can also pick up mannequin-style jewellery stands very cheaply. These will not be anatomically proportionate like the traditional full-size and scaled-down dress forms, but may be close enough to give you an impression of what your garment will be like.

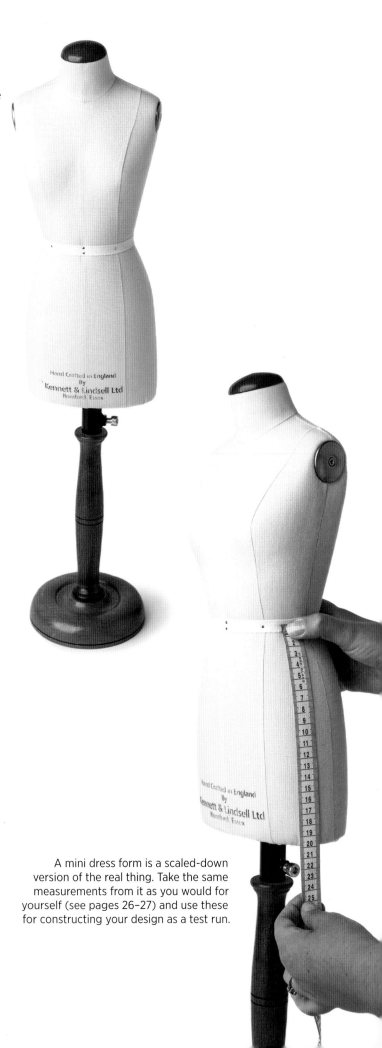

Your sewing machine

As long as your sewing machine has a few basic stitches such as a straight stitch, zigzag and straight stretch stitch that you can vary in length or width you are more than good to go!

A sewing machine with a buttonhole stitch is very handy and quick but not essential, as you can replicate it with a well-practised zigzag stitch. Your machine will generally come with a selection of sewing feet. These will, of course, make the job easier, so check your manual for using the correct sewing feet for your stitches and fabrics.

An overlocker/serger is something you might purchase to treat yourself, but you don't necessarily need one, as most sewing machines have a mock overlocking stitch... That being said, when you do get one, it's a game changer. An overlocker/serger cuts the fabric as it sews; there isn't much room for error, but it makes you look like a semi-professional seamstress with your garments finished and sewn to perfection, even if you still feel like you're a beginner.

A mini dress form is a scaled-down version of the real thing. Take the same measurements from it as you would for yourself (see pages 26–27) and use these for constructing your design as a test run.

DRESSMAKING ESSENTIALS

Interfacing

Interfacing is your best friend when it comes to dressmaking... and you might not have even heard of it or used it before. But when you do, it really makes a difference to the look, feel and wear of a garment. It is either fused or sewn into the unseen parts of a garment and adds structure and support to construction and design details. Interfacing is most commonly white but may also be black, grey or flesh-coloured.

Interfacing is not a one-size-fits-all product: it's important to match your interfacing weight to the weight of your fabric. As a general rule, I like to think of interfacing as an invisible friend; it shouldn't alter the 'feel' of the fabric too much. For example, in areas such as facings and plackets, you want the fabric to be strengthened, but not so much that the fabric feels stiff. Generally, the only time this rule doesn't apply is in an area such as a waistband; you want your interfacing to be a lot firmer here, so that it provides the structure and support a waistband needs. It's good to have a selection of different weights so that you can choose the right interfacing for different parts of your garment and for a range of fabrics.

Fastenings

Buttons are the jewels of any sewing kit. I have so many jars and biscuit tins filled with treasured, vintage, hand-me-down and new buttons! I've even been known to spend the odd afternoon cutting the buttons off old clothes that are to be recycled or upcycled. Many will probably never be used, but I'm sure, like me, my daughter will love to sort through them when she is older.

It's also good to keep a stash of zips. A selection of lengths and colours is a must. Whether plastic or metal-toothed, closed or open-ended, decorative or invisible, zips will always come in handy.

A selection of fastenings like hooks-and-eyes and snap fasteners are also very useful to have in your stash and can help with those finishing touches on areas like waistbands and facings.

Threads

This sounds like an obvious item to have in your sewing kit – and you wouldn't get far without it! – but I still wanted to mention sewing thread and give you some tips. Having a selection of different threads can make a lot of difference. Not only will you want to match your thread colour to your fabric (or use a contrasting colour!), you may need to match the type of thread, too. For instance, if you are making something out of 100 per cent cotton you may want to use cotton thread rather than an all-purpose polyester thread. Although you may not notice the difference during the sew, when it comes to washing your garment later the different types of materials may react in different ways and you may get some funny results if one shrinks more than the other, for example.

Top tip

Use a cheaper thread for tailor tacking or sewing up a toile, as cheaper thread will be easier to pull or break out at speed – saving you time and leaving your chosen thread for the garment.

DRAFTING TOOLS

You might find that you have a lot of these tools already, so you may not need to get anything additional. Here are a few essential items that you will need when drafting your own pattern.

Drafting paper

Dressmaking paper can come in different formats: on a roll and purchased in metres or yards, or in pre-cut sheets in packs. It can be plain or printed with grids or dots and crosses. If you can, try some out to see which you prefer – some people find that the grid or dot-and-cross paper speed things up a little, as they give you the benefit of marked-out squares ready for use, but others find the marks a little confusing.

If you are struggling to get hold of dressmaking paper, I would recommend using wallpaper lining or greaseproof paper instead – your paper needs to be hardwearing but thin enough to be able to trace through.

Cardboard

It is a good idea to make a 'hard copy' of your basic block (see pages 28–31). Traditionally you would use manilla card, which is brown in colour and is hardwearing. It needs to be, as you will be tracing around this basic block shape for each new design rather than creating a new basic block every time. If you want to start off by making practise skirts in miniature, A4 (21 x 30cm/8¼ x 11¾in) coloured craft card is ideal.

Sharp pencil, sharpener and eraser

You need to make clear, crisp lines with your pencil and we all make mistakes, so these really are integral to the job.

Felt-tip pens

I like to go over my lines after I have drawn out my block and clearly mark the front and the back patterns, along with all the other relevant pattern markings such as darts and notches. I would suggest using at least two colours.

Metre ruler

Not essential but it really does make the job quick and easy – especially if you are going to make long skirts!

Calculator

Why get brain-freeze trying to do the maths in your head? There is not a lot of arithmetic involved here, but it is essential to be accurate so it's worth grabbing one or using your smartphone.

Paper scissors

Nice, sharp paper scissors are a must, especially when you start cutting and manipulating your blocks to create fabulous shapes and designs!

Sticky tape

You will need this to piece patterns together when we start manipulating and cutting into the basic blocks.

Tracing wheel

This is not essential, but it does help if you can't quite see through the drafting paper when tracing off. This tool is like a pizza cutter, but instead of cutting it makes small indents through the paper. It can also be used with dressmaking tracing paper for marking out patterns directly onto fabric, as well as with patterns that you cannot cut up.

Pattern master ruler
with 45-degree and 90-degree markings

As we are going to be drawing square and rectangular shapes it's important that we get the angles correct!

French curve

This tool provides a quick and easy way to make consistent and accurate curves; bear in mind that it is not essential as, with a little practice, you can learn to do this freehand!

Toile fabric

Traditionally your toile ('test garment') fabric would be canvas or calico, but an old bed sheet can work just as well. If your skirt is going to be made from fabric that you have not used before, or that is a very different weight or feel to the toile, it might be wise to make your toile using a similar but inexpensive material, so that it is as close to the 'real' thing as possible. This way you can practise your fabric handling beforehand.

Marking tools

When making a toile, you really want to be able to see your adjustments so you can transfer them easily onto your block pattern later. Therefore, if using a bed sheet or calico to toile with I like to use a laundry pen. This way I know the marks are not going to erase with unpicking and overhandling. If I'm using a different fabric but think I'll be able to actually wear the toile afterwards because the adjustments are minimal, then I use a water-erasable pen instead. Make sure you do a test on a scrap of fabric beforehand, in case the water-erasable pen doesn't actually come out properly.

FABRICOLOGY

What fabric should I make my skirt from?

When thinking about what kind of fabric I want to sew with, I think about clothes that I already own. Whether you realize it or not, you already have a wealth of fabric knowledge because you wear clothes every day. In the summer months, you reach for dresses or shirts that will probably be made from a light cotton or silk. Likewise, when you are cold, you grab a jumper that may be fleeced or knitted or you wear heavy corduroy or denim trousers to keep you warm. Upcycling old clothes to make new garments helped me to build my fabric knowledge. In cutting up what I no longer wore, I got to handle so many different types of fabric – plus I knew how to care for them because they come with a washing and information label attached to them.

When buying fabric, think about how it feels in your hands. Chances are you have something similar in your wardrobe. What garment is it? When do you wear it? Does the fabric feel right for the project you are making? Check how the fabric flows – is it stiff or does it drape? Is it heavy or light? If it is on a roll, ask if you can unravel a little of it to check this. Put the fabric against you to see if the colour or pattern suits you. You may love looking at it but will you really wear it? Give it a light pull – does it stretch? Fabric is constructed in two different ways – woven or knitted – and these behave very differently to one another. Woven fabrics tend to be more rigid compared to knitted fabrics, which stretch. All these factors need to be considered when using fabric and making a garment.

Keep a fabric diary

I like to keep a fabric diary. I sew little leftover scraps of fabric into a book with a note on what I was making, when and who for, as well as notes on what the fabric is and how to care for it – plus any tips that I came across as I was sewing the project. Building up this kind of resource can help you choose fabric for future projects.

Where do I get fabric from?

Your home: old linens or bedsheets are great to use as there is so much fabric in them. They are a cheap source of pre-washed fabric that will help you to get started, whether making a toile or for a finished garment.

Charity or thrift shops: when you have exhausted your home and the homes of your family and friends, the charity shop is a great place to try next. I have come across some amazing retro-printed linen and fabric in charity shops, not to mention buttons and trims. They can be a treasure chest of goodies and you're also giving to a good cause!

Local markets: I'm very lucky to live near Birmingham's notorious Rag Market. It's a vault of fabric delights and if you ever get the chance to go, please do! But even in smaller towns, you may find the occasional fabric stall on market days. I love visiting my hometown of West Bromwich – because of the culturally diverse residents, you get a wonderful array of fabric choices at very low prices. You can always find some amazing bargains, but always check the quality of the fabric and print, check for imperfections and marks, and always buy an extra half metre (half yard) or so, in case you need to avoid any areas. Don't be afraid to haggle if you are buying a few different pieces from the same stall.

Local haberdasheries: it really is worth doing an internet search to find your local haberdashery. Not only will they stock fabric and sewing equipment, but they are also an invaluable source of knowledge. My local haberdashery is super-helpful and always willing to give me sewing advice and a slice of cake. I cannot promise you will get cake at every haberdashery, but I'm very sure that you will always find someone who can help – you just need to ask!

National sewing events: imagine all the haberdashery stores in the world, all under one roof. Yep, it's kinda like that, so bring a trolley. Going to these events can make for a very long day, so go prepared! You will be in fabric and haberdashery heaven with so much to choose from, as well as sewing workshops to take part in – these are places to find inspiration and new trends.

Online: with technology at your fingertips, you can easily buy fabric from all over the world. If you don't get the chance to dedicate an afternoon to go fabric shopping in person, then online can be a good option. As well as using your search engine, check out Pinterest, Facebook and Instagram too. I have found some wonderful independent online shops though social media, so get browsing. The only downside to online shopping is that you don't get to feel the fabric first, and that's my favourite part.

Looking after your fabric

Washing fabric: the first thing you will need to do is wash your fabric. You don't want to spend time sewing a skirt that then shrinks in the wash. Some fabrics will come pre-shrunk and of course upcycled linen will already have been washed, but it's always best to give them a quick cycle in the washing machine. Vintage or old fabrics will also need to be tested with a quick cycle, as they may not stand up to washing – fibres do weaken over time and you don't want to get all excited about a vintage make just to have it fall apart on you.

Ironing vs pressing: once you have washed and dried your fabric you will need to give it a good iron and then a press: there is a difference between the two! Ironing a garment is what you do at home – moving the iron back and forth over the garment until you get the light creases out. Pressing is different. You need to hold the iron over an area like a dart or seam, apply a little pressure and possibly steam and then lift away. You are setting something in place and if pressing is done correctly then it should be still visible after several washes. When ironing, be careful of fabrics that are manmade or have textured surfaces like velvet or corduroy. You don't want to melt or flatten these fabrics, so use a pressing cloth to protect the fabric when pressing, and always iron a test piece of fabric first. Fold your fabric with the selvedge/selvage edges and the wrong sides together and press in a fold. This will make it easier to work with.

Storing fabric: fold your fabric into squares or rectangles until you get to the size you need for storing, rather than scrunching it up. Not only is this a space saver, it will save you a job trying to get the creases out when you are ready to sew. Once you have washed, pressed and folded your fabric, try to store it in a dry and dark place, or at least out of direct sunlight. Sunlight, over time, will cause damage to your fabric by fading it.

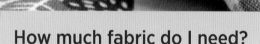

How much fabric do I need?

Several factors will influence how much fabric you will need for a project:

- How tall are you?
- What size are you?
- Does the fabric have a pattern repeat?
- What is the fabric width?

Another way of thinking about it is: how long is the skirt you want to make? If it is a full-length skirt, then a good gauge would be to double this length, as you have a front and a back to a skirt, then add a little extra for seams and hems or to pattern match.

As you are drafting your own skirt patterns, you have the advantage of testing out the design with a toile first (pages 32–37). So, to find out exactly how much fabric you will need for your design, place your unpicked toile along the floor, making sure your pattern pieces don't go outside the fabric width. Once all your pattern pieces are laid out as if they were sitting on the fabric, measure the length you require.

If your fabric choice has an obvious repeating pattern, you will need to measure the repeat and add that to your fabric measurement too, to ensure you can pattern match correctly.

As a very general rule of thumb, I always buy 3m (3¼ yd) of fabric as this will cover most garments. Any leftover fabric will always end up in other projects.

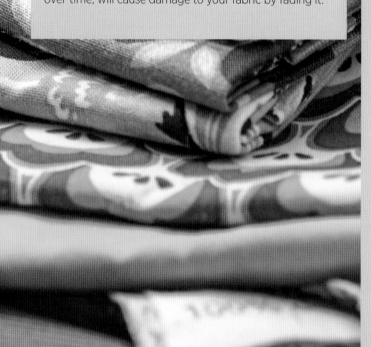

Positioning and cutting out your pattern pieces

If you have never made garments before, positioning and cutting your pattern pieces out of fabric can be the scariest part. But, by following a few simple rules, you will feel more confident with each slice of the scissors.

• Fold your fabric with the right sides together along the grainline first (see explanation, right), making sure the fabric is not twisting and has no creases.

• Match your grainlines by measuring at intervals from the pattern's grainline to the fabric's grainline (folded edge or selvedge), ensuring that both are parallel and in line with each other (shown below).

• Be aware of seam allowances and pattern pieces cut on the fold. Not all pattern pieces are placed along the folded edge. Also be mindful that your basic block does not have seam allowances included, so you will need to either add these to the paper pattern first or to the fabric directly, therefore don't place the patterns too close together.

• Secure the pattern pieces in place with dressmaking pins or weights before cutting out.

• Cut with smooth, long cuts rather than shorter, sharp motions, which will disturb the fabric and potentially cause cutting errors.

• Make sure you transfer all the pattern markings or notches to the fabric with either tailor's tacks or chalk before removing the pattern pieces.

Fabric terminology

Grainline: runs lengthways down the fabric and is created by the vertical warp threads (see below). When you are positioning patterns onto fabric, imagine that the grainline will run from your head to toe down the garment.

Cross grain: runs across the fabric and is created by the horizontal weft threads (see below).

Selvedge/selvage: the raw edge of the fabric that is created by the ends of the cross grain; it runs parallel to your grainline (see below).

Bias: if you cut at a 45-degree angle to your cross grain and grainline, this is known as the bias (see below). For a dramatic or draped shape, patterns will be placed and cut along the bias because of the stretch qualities it gives you.

Notches: marks that you make in fabric for points of reference when sewing.

Nap: this is the raised texture of a fabric. Textured fabric such as velvet will need to be handled differently to cottons: you will need to make sure that the direction of the nap is going the same way through all your pattern pieces, otherwise they will look different in colour.

Seam allowance: this is the distance between the edge of the fabric and your stitch line. Seam allowances can vary from pattern to pattern and as you are creating your own skirt pattern, you can set this distance yourself.

Hem: a hem is a way of finishing off your raw edges. Hems can be found at the bottom of skirts (and trousers and cuffs). They can be single (folded once) or double (folded twice).

Ease: this is the difference between your body measurement and the finished garment's size. Ease is added to your body measurements when making a garment. A tighter garment will have less ease compared to a loose-fitting garment.

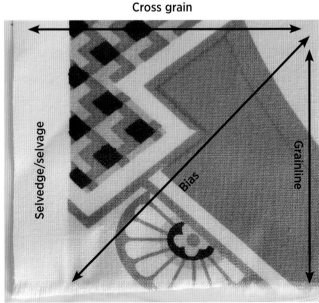

Cross grain

Selvedge/selvage

Bias

Grainline

Seam finishings

To construct your skirts you will be sewing pieces of fabric together to create seams. There are lots of methods you can use to do this and which seam you use may depend on the fabric you're working with as well as the purpose of the seam.

A **plain seam** is the most common and simple seam. We will be using this method a lot. It is created by putting the right sides of the fabric together and joining them with a stitched line, leaving you with two seam allowances that will need to be pressed open (as shown) or to one side. We will be using the plain seam to construct your toile, although your stitch length will need to be increased to create this temporary seam, as you can then unpick and adjust the toile more easily this way.

It is always a good idea to finish your seams, especially if the seams are exposed, as with the plain seam (you won't need to finish your toile seams though). **Pinking, overlocking** or **zigzag stitching** are all good ways to finish a seam. If you do not finish your seams, the fabric will begin to fray as you wear and wash it. Over time this may affect the stitches and your garment may fall apart.

A **French seam** is a great one to use if you are sewing fine fabrics that fray. It looks like a plain seam from the front, but the raw seams are enclosed. You do this by placing the *wrong* sides together first and sewing the seam line. You then refold the fabric so that the right sides are facing and sew again, enclosing all the raw edges inside the seam.

A **flat-fell seam** is a very strong seam that you will find on items like jeans. It is created by folding one raw seam under, trapping the other one and is secured with a second line of parallel stitching. This is a great seam finish that can be sewn on all fabrics.

A **welt seam** is very similar to a flat-fell seam. Instead of tucking one seam under before sewing, with a welt seam you just trim one seam allowance and neaten the other one. Press the neatened seam allowance over the trimmed one and then topstitch in place.

Enclosed seams can be found on pockets and facings. You won't need to finish the seam but you will need to trim it to reduce bulk; if it is a curved seam, you will need to clip the seams by cutting V-shapes into them. This will allow the curve to lie flat and reduce bulk.

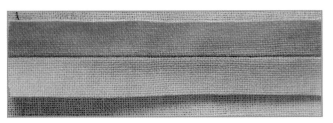

Plain seam

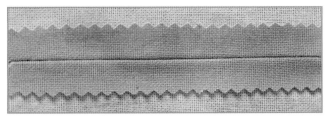

Pinked finish

French seam

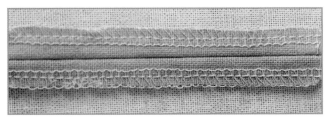

Overlocked finish

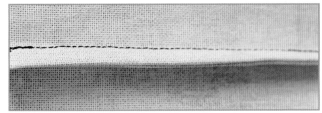

Flat-fell seam

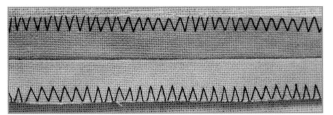

Zigzag finish

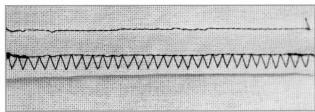

Welt seam

YOUR BODY, YOUR BLOCK

We all come in different shapes and sizes –
we are all unique! And it's certainly not as
simple as being a different 'size' on a scale
of 0–24. Let's face it – you might be a
certain size in one shop, but from my
experience that's no guarantee you'll be
the same 'number' everywhere else!

I want to feel confident in my own
skin and not be constricted by my
clothes. Making garments using your
own body measurements is one way
of achieving this. It's your unique body, so
make your own unique block and your
own unique clothes to fit it!

WHAT IS A BLOCK?

A block is the starting point from which all clothes patterns are made – including skirts, bodices, dresses and trousers. Blocks come in standard sizes as you would find in high-street clothes. In this book, however, we are going to be using your body measurements to create your very own, made-to-measure block. Once we have drawn out your block, it will produce a very basic shape. To the right you can see the paper blocks for the front and back of my skirt pinned to muslin, ready to make a toile. To check that our block works, we will make a toile first before we cut into, manipulate and alter the block to design a huge number of different skirt styles.

WHAT IS A TOILE?

A toile is the first version of your garment and it is best to make it up in an inexpensive fabric (see page 17). I tend to use bed sheets, as they are cheap and easy to get hold of; traditionally, fabrics such as muslin or calico are used.

A toile will not have any fixtures or closures like zips or buttons. It is just a quick sew-up of the pattern block you have created, so that you can try it on before going to the next stage (see the image below).

A toile will highlight any alterations that need to be made to your block. Your toile should follow the contours of your body and should be fairly close-fitting. Any adjustments made to the toile will need to be transferred back to the block for future reference (see pages 35–37).

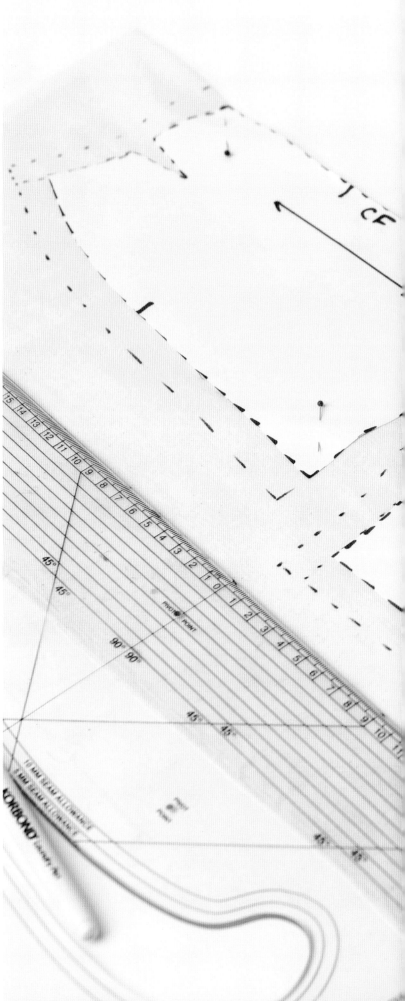

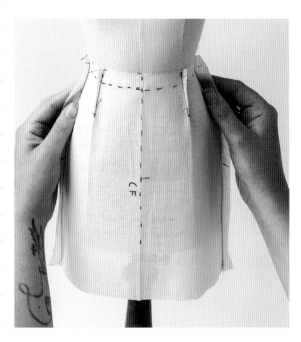

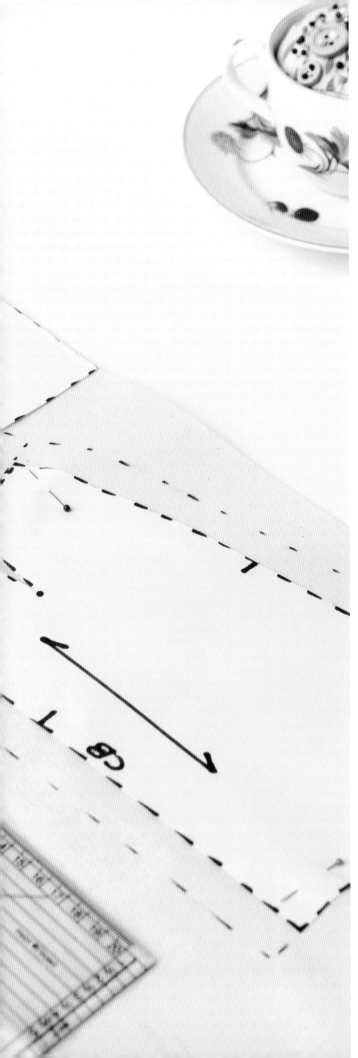

WHAT DETAILS SHOULD I INCLUDE?

Centre front (CF) and centre back (CB)

A block is normally only made up of half a front and half a back, and these won't be the same shape. So it is crucial to remind yourself which is which when it comes to positioning your pattern onto fabric or adding seam allowances. I like to use different colour pens: blue for the front, red for the back.

Seam allowances (SA)

Blocks do not come with seam or hem allowances, because how much we add and where depends on your design. To remind myself, I write 'no SA' on my blocks, otherwise I tend to go into autopilot, cut out the fabric and then wonder why my garment is too small. Remember, you are drafting your *block* to your exact finished size; you need to add seam allowances to the *pattern*, so that the finished skirt fits.

Fit lines   - - - - - - - - -

Fit lines relate to your bust, waist and hips (although we won't be worrying about busts in this book). I also like to add the centre front and back to this list as all these points help to check the fit of the block when wearing the toile. It's important that we know where these fit lines are so that we can ensure, for example, that the hipline is sitting on your actual hip. It's also important that when we do make adjustments, we transfer these back to the block at the right places (see pages 35–37).

Notches   — ● ▲

Notches are marks we make on our block and patterns, and can be as simple as a small line, dot or triangle, and can be used in combination with each other. Notches help you to accurately align pieces together. This will be especially important if you are adding darts, pleats or pockets. It is important that you transfer all your notches from your block to the pattern and from your pattern to your fabric before removing your pattern, to ensure that all positions are the same and haven't moved.

Grainlines   ⟷

This helps you place the pattern correctly in relation to the fabric's grain (see page 20). For our basic block, the grainline will be parallel to the centre front and centre back. For the majority of the skirt recipes the grainline is unaltered, however, a pattern's grainline can be altered so that the pieces are cut on the bias; the pattern is positioned at a 45-degree angle to the fabric's grainline. Cutting on the bias will give a woven fabric more movement and flexibility, so a flared skirt cut on the bias will really swing and sway. Whatever the orientation of the grainline, make sure you mark it on your patterns for future reference.

TAKING YOUR OWN MEASUREMENTS

Now this may sound like the daunting bit but we actually only need four measurements to make your skirt block. To get started you are going to need a few bits and pieces...

Firstly, you are going to need a fitting buddy, and I'm not talking about a friend. All you need is a length of elastic. Tie a length of elastic around your waist and leave it! That's the important part – resist the temptation to adjust it by pulling it down. We want the elastic to find your true waist. If you feel like you are constantly pulling down tops or dresses, that's because your garment doesn't fit you correctly and is trying to find your true waistline. So, let the elastic do its job and don't be shocked if you find that your true waistline is actually about 5cm (2in) above your belly button.

You are also going to need a full-length mirror, a tape measure and a pen and paper. The most important thing here is to be honest. No one else needs to know these numbers, so write down your true measurements. Don't pull the tape measure too tight or too loose, as the correct ease will be added in later. Most importantly of all: remember to breathe easily and don't hold your breath.

Top tips

1. Avoid wearing several layers when measuring yourself – we don't want to be adding unnecessary inches now, do we?

2. Try to ensure that the tape measure is parallel to the floor in the front and the back by checking in the mirror.

3. Try to look in the mirror when taking the measurements and avoid bending and twisting to read the tape measure as this will alter your size and shape as you move. By looking in the mirror you will see if you are slouching or altering your natural stance.

1. Natural waistline

Measure where your elastic is sitting. This is your true waist. Don't suck your tummy in – a comfortable, true fit is actally more flattering.

2. Hipline

This is not where your hip bone is, we are looking for the fullest part of your bottom. Remember to keep your tape measure parallel to the floor by checking in the mirror.

3. Waist to desired length

With the start of the tape measure facing down towards to floor, adjust the tape measure to the length you want. With your fingers, pinch the tape measure at the waist point and move it away from your body to take the reading.

4. Waist to hip

Measure from your waist to where you took your hip measurement. Look in the mirror to get the measurement; avoid looking down as this will alter your shape.

YOUR BODY, YOUR BLOCK

HOW TO DRAW OUT YOUR OWN BLOCK

This may look a little strange but we are going to be drawing your basic skirt block into a square/rectangle shape. Within the square you will have both the front and back part of your skirt.

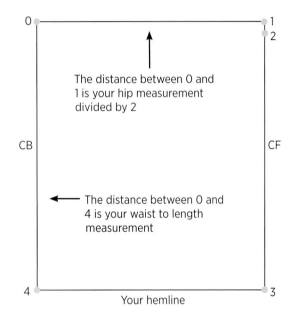

The distance between 0 and 1 is your hip measurement divided by 2

The distance between 0 and 4 is your waist to length measurement

Your hemline

1 First of all, roll or iron out a sheet of drafting paper, about 1m (1 yd) long – you need to make sure it is longer than your waist to length measurement by at least 30cm (12in).

2 In the top left-hand corner, mark point 0.

3 Draw a line across to the top right-hand corner using your hip calculation. This is point 1.

4 With the right-angle on your pattern master, square down from point 0 using your waist to length measurement to create point 4 (this line will be your centre back), and from point 1 to create point 3 (this line will be your centre front).

5 Join points 3 and 4 together to create your hemline. Double-check the distance is correct – it should be the same as from point 0 to point 1 (your hip calculation).

6 Along the line between points 1 and 3, mark out your balance factor measurement: point 2.

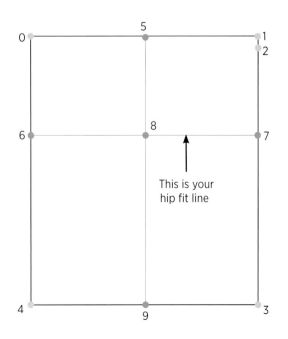

This is your hip fit line

7 Along the line between points 0 and 4, mark out your waist to hip measurement to create point 6.

8 Along the line between points 1 and 3, mark out your waist to hip measurement to create point 7 – the line between points 6 and 7 is your hip fit line.

9 Mark the centre point of the hip fit line as point 8.

10 Mark the centre point of the line between points 0 and 1 to create point 5, then mark the centre point of the line between points 4 and 3 to create point 9. Draw a line through to connect points 5, 8 and 9.

11 To create points 10 and 11, measure out twice the balance factor, either side of point 5.

12 To create ease around the hipline, take your hip calculation and add 2.5cm (1in) before dividing by 2. Measure out from point 6 towards point 7 and mark this measurement. Repeat from point 7 towards point 6. You will have created a mark either side of point 8.

13 From point 9, measure 5cm (2in) to the left to create point 12 and repeat on the other side to create point 13.

14 Using your tailor's curve, draw a curved line that joins point 10 with the mark just to the right of point 8.

15 From this point, continue to draw down to point 13 using a straight line.

16 Using your tailor's curve, draw a curved line that joins point 11 with the mark just to the left of point 8. From this point, continue to draw down to point 12 using a straight line.

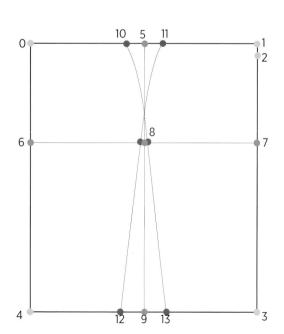

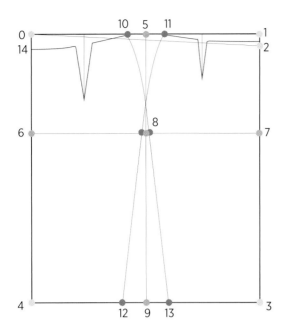

17 Add 5mm (¼in) to the balance factor and measure down from point 0 to create point 14.

18 To create the shape of the skirt top, connect point 14 to point 10 using your tailor's curve. Repeat to connect point 11 and point 2.

19 Measure between points 0 and 10 and points 11 and 1 and add the two measurements together. To find the surplus amount, work out the difference between this calculation and half your actual waist measurement before subtracting 1cm (³/₈in) to allow for ease.

20 Using the surplus calculation, we need to create two dart measurements: one-third for the front dart and two-thirds for the back dart. Find the mid-point between points 0 and 10 and square down about 13cm (5in) to create the point of the dart. Distribute your back dart calculation (two-thirds of your surplus) where the square down meets the curve.

21 Find the mid-point between points 1 and 5, and this time square down 9cm (3½in) for the point of the dart. Distribute your front dart calculation in the same way.

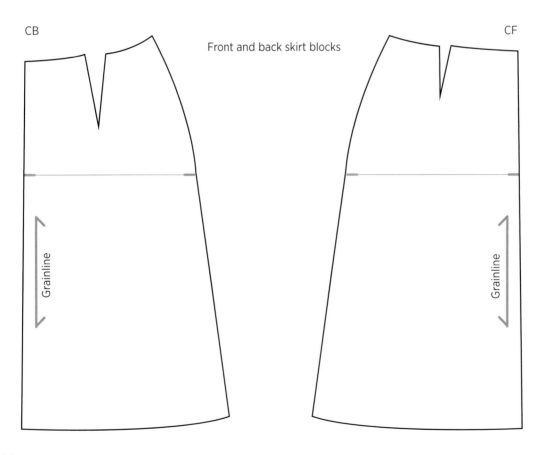

Front and back skirt blocks

22 You have now finished drafting your skirt block. To make tracing off easier, use your coloured felt pens to highlight the front and back skirt patterns (see the photo on page 29). Trace off the front and back skirt patterns individually, so they no longer cross in the centre of the square. Mark out clearly the centre front (CF) and centre back (CB), hipline, dart positions and finally the grainline, which is parallel to your CF and CB.

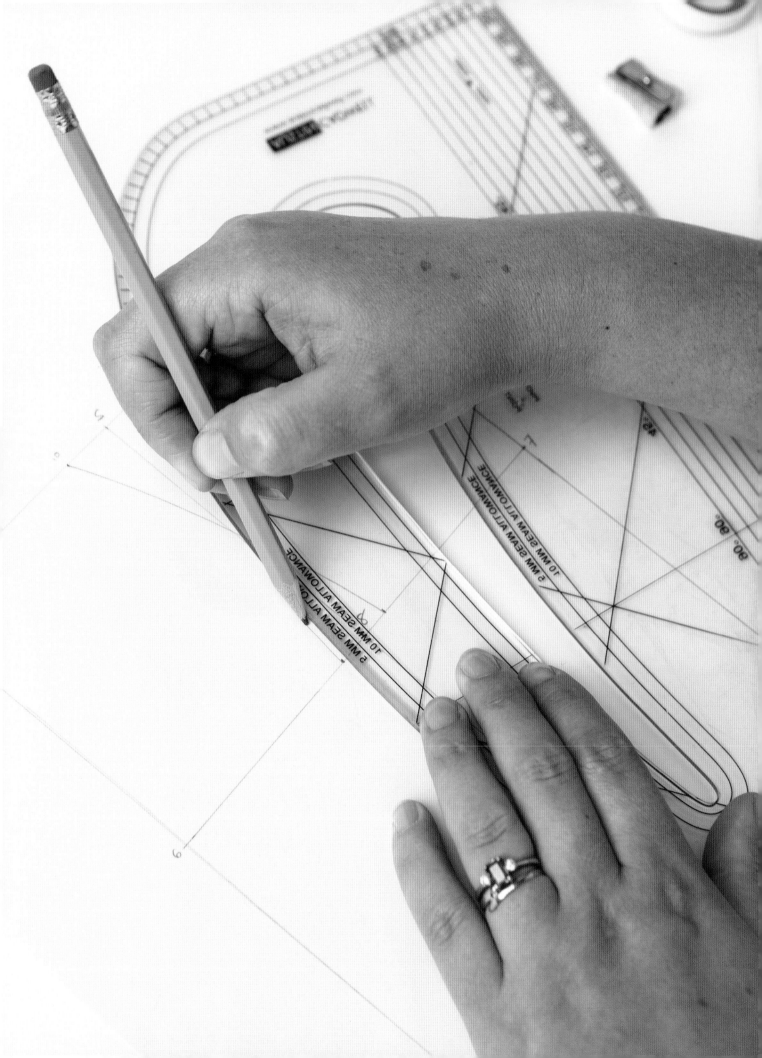

MAKING A TOILE AND CHECKING THE FIT

Remember that a toile is a practice make, so don't use your best fabrics for this step. We are simply going to make up your basic block to ensure that everything fits in the right places. We won't be adding any details like pockets or fixtures at this stage, so it's a quick process that will help ensure your skirt is going to look and fit fabulously.

Creating your fabric pieces

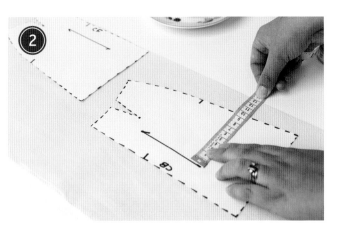

1 For the purpose of the toile we want to cut your skirt front on the fold of the fabric. This will create one symmetrical piece rather than two separate pieces that we would need to stitch back together again. However, your skirt back *will* need to consist of two cut and sewn halves, so that you can get in and out of your toile. Fold your fabric in half along the grainline; place your front pattern piece onto the fold. Place your back pattern piece away from the folded edge and either adjacent to or below the front pattern piece. As your fabric is folded you will end up cutting out two mirrored back pieces with the one cut.

2 You need to make sure that you pin your pattern pieces in line with the grainline of the fabric. A simple way to check this is to take your measuring tape and measure at intervals between the grainline marked on the pattern and the folded edge of the fabric – the measurement should be the same all the way down.

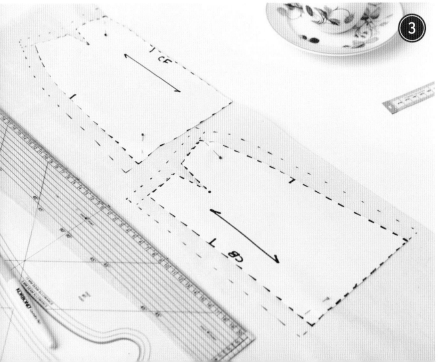

3 With your pieces pinned in place, it's time to think about your seam allowances, as these pattern pieces do not have seam allowances included. You will need to add a seam allowance of 1.5cm (⅝in) onto the outer edges of your pattern pieces – the exceptions to this are the centre front, which is currently placed on the fold, and the hemlines, as these will be added later once we decide on the finished fit and length.

Top tip

If you are worried about fit around the waist and tummy area, I would increase your seam allowance to 2cm (¾in) at the side seam only, so you have more fabric to make adjustments if needed.

4 Cut your fabric pieces out around your seam allowance marks. Make a note of where the hipline is on your fabric by either making a small notch within the seam allowance, or marking it on in pen (see tip box, right).

5 If it is difficult to tell which is the right or wrong side of the fabric then use your preferred marking tool to make a mark on the fabric. This way you will now know which is which.

6 Mark the tips of your darts into the fabric using either tailor's tacks, or your preferred marking tool. A tailor's tack is a loose, looping hand-stitch that, when cut, leaves a loop of thread in both pieces of fabric.

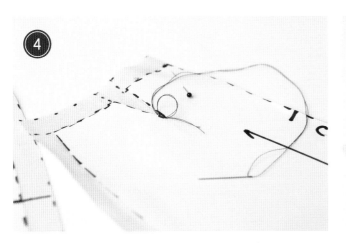

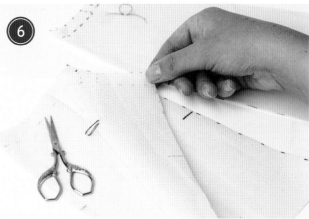

Top tip

When using calico, I like to use a laundry pen when marking my dart and hip positions, so that I know these marks are not going to disappear as I work on or press my toile. If there is a possibility that you might want to keep your toile as a garment because you have used a cheap but pretty fabric, definitely don't use a laundry pen as the marks will not come out! I have many a toile that has gone on to be part of my wardrobe staples. Bonus!

7 Remove the paper patterns from your fabric.

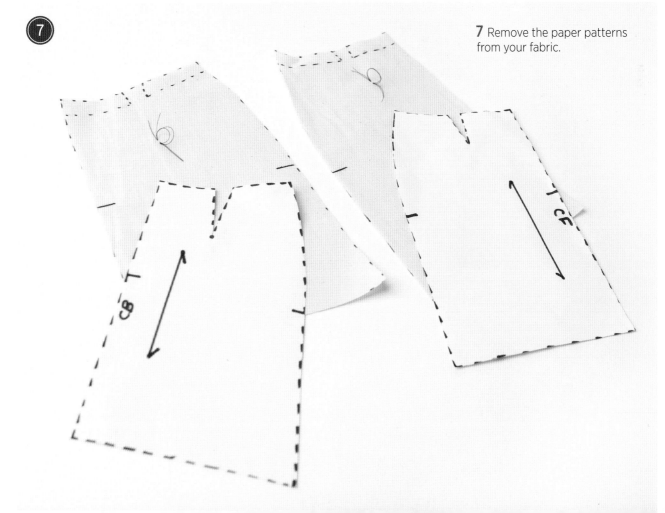

Sewing up

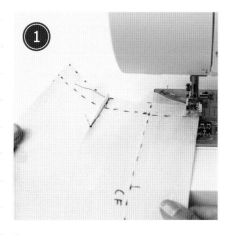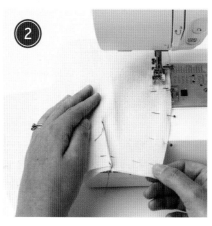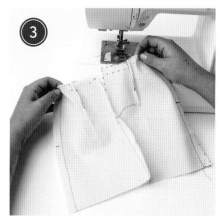

1 Pinch together the fabric at the darts, right sides facing, and sew from the edge of the fabric to the tip of the dart, where your tailor's tack or mark is. Sew your darts into place on the front and back pieces, but don't remove the tailor's tacks or marks yet.

2 With the right sides together, pin the left back and front side seams together, making sure the hip notches or marks match. Stitch together. Repeat on the other side.

3 Sew the centre-back seam together but only sew up as far as the hipline, as we need to be able to try the skirt on. At the hipline, sew a small backstitch so that your stitching doesn't come undone in the fitting. Remember that as this is a toile you won't need to add a waistband or hem it.

> *Top tip*
> Increase your stitch length on your sewing machine; the stitches will be quick and easy to unpick if we need to make any changes later.

Checking the fit

Now it's time to check the fit. Before you try the skirt on, make sure that the hipline measurement and the seam allowance on the waistband are clearly visible, so that you can easily see how the skirt will fit.

1 Try the skirt on inside out. If we need to make changes to the darts then we need to be able to access them. If you are on your own, your full-length mirror is going to be your fitting buddy. Pin the remaining back seam together first – do this at the front and then spin the skirt around. Once you are in the skirt, try not to look down to check the fit – look in the mirror and stand naturally.

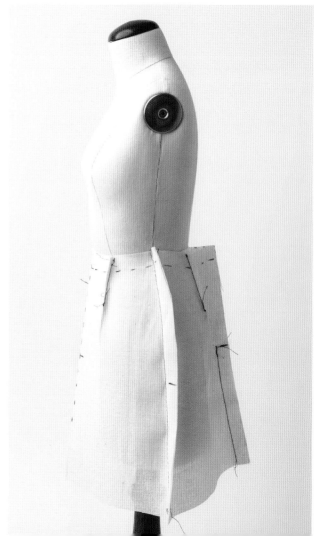

2 Firstly, assess the shape around your hips. Are the hip curves in the skirt in the right place on your body?

3 Do the darts feel and look comfortable against your tummy and lower back? Do we need to let them out a little or take more fabric away? Remember you have to allow for a little ease here so you can breathe and sit comfortably.

4 The sit test! Try sitting down, but be careful of the centre-back pins! Is the skirt too tight across your legs and hips? If any of these measurements don't feel quite right, read on to find out how to correct them...

> *Top tip*
>
> The instructions below are a guide for taking things in (to make smaller). If you need to take things out (make larger), unpick the relevant seams, whether a pair of darts (front or back) or the side seams, repin, and continue as given below. Remember to adjust evenly across both seams, allow for a little ease and to check the fit with a sit test!

Adjusting a side seam

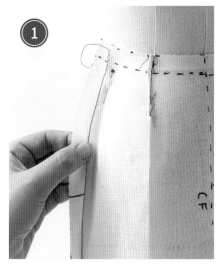

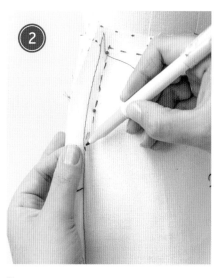

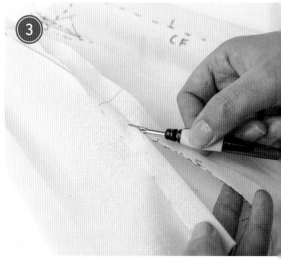

1 Pinch the fabric at the side seam so that it fits correctly against your body; insert a few pins to keep the fabric in place. You'll need to do this a little at a time on both sides, so that the skirt remains symmetrical.

2 Redraw the corrected lines using a marking pen. Take the skirt off, restitch the new side seams and then try the skirt back on to ensure that the fit is now correct. Once you are happy with the fit you will need to transfer the changes to your original paper pattern.

3 Unpick your stitches – this should be easy if you lengthened your stitches.

continued overleaf

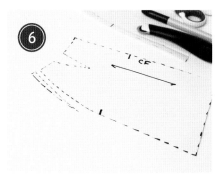

4 Use a tracing wheel to transfer the changes to your paper pattern – align the fabric on top of the paper pattern and 'draw' over the new seam line.

5 You can see here the new seam line.

6 Cut away the excess from the pattern. If you have no further adjustments to make, you are ready to start designing your perfect skirt!

Adjusting a dart

1 Pinch the fabric at the dart so that it fits correctly against your body; insert a few pins to keep the fabric in place. You'll need to do this a little at a time on both sides, so that the skirt remains symmetrical. Note that if the skirt is too tight around the tummy, you will need to unpick the darts first, before repinning the dart to a more comfortable position.

2 Redraw the corrected lines using a marking pen. Take the skirt off, and check the new darts are symmetrical before restitching them. Try the skirt back on to ensure that the fit is now correct. Once you are happy with the fit we will need to transfer the changes to your original paper pattern.

3 Unpick your stitches – this should be easy if you lengthened your stitches. Use a tracing wheel to transfer the changes to your paper pattern – align the fabric on top of the paper pattern and 'draw' over the new dart lines.

4 Cut away the excess from the pattern. If you have no further adjustments to make, you are ready to start designing your perfect skirt!

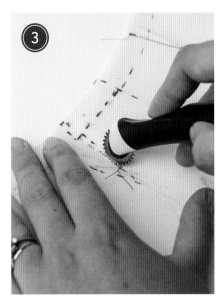

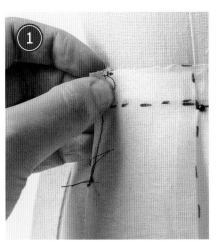

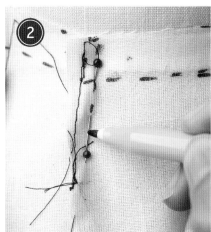

Adjusting the waistline

1 If you want to lower the waistline, work out where you want your skirt to sit and measure and mark this at intervals around the top of your skirt. Remember that the current marks are the stitching line, so this could be the edge of your skirt's facing or the beginning of the waistband.

2 Your new waistline without a seam allowance.

3 Unpick your stitches – this should be easy if you lengthened your stitches. Use a tracing wheel to transfer the changes to your paper pattern – align the fabric on top of the paper pattern and 'draw' over the new waistline.

4 Cut away the excess from the pattern. If you have no further adjustments to make, you are ready to start designing your perfect skirt!

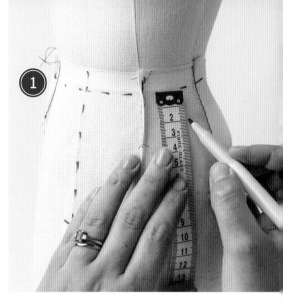

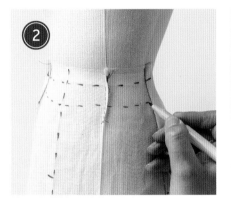

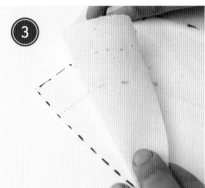

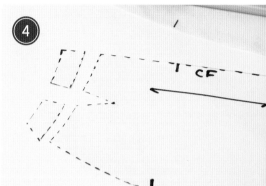

CREATING YOUR SKIRT

Now you have drafted your basic skirt block and checked the fit, we can start to get creative by doing a number of things to this base pattern. These have been separated into three categories for you.

1. Skirt shapes (see pages 38–51)

This is the starting point for your skirt and will include structural elements like adding pleats, closing darts and adding flare.

2. Fastenings and fixtures (see pages 52–65)

This section gives you a choice on how you are going to get in and out of your skirt, covering practical elements like waistbands, facings, zips and button fronts.

3. Details and finishings (see pages 66–83)

These are the extras that make your skirt totally unique. Here we will be covering design elements like yokes, pockets and bound hems.

SKIRT SHAPES

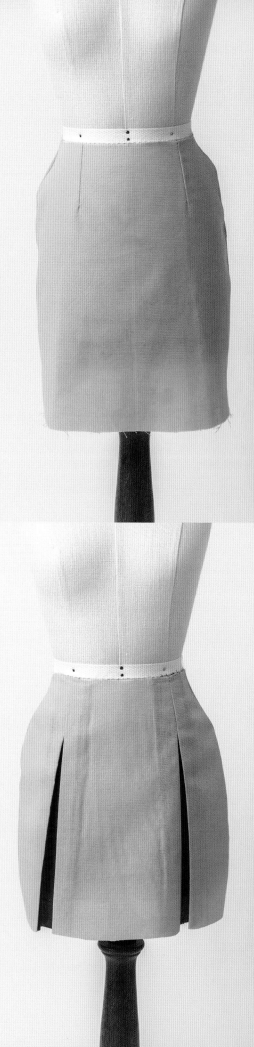

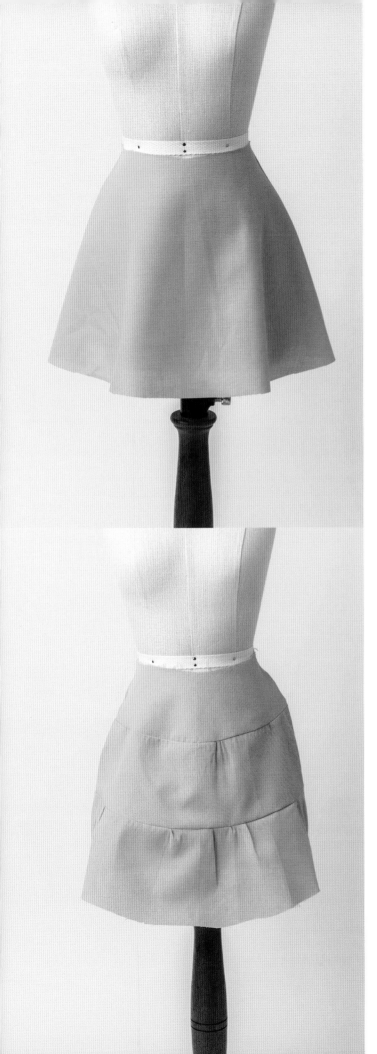

When designing your skirt, you first need to pick a shape. There are many options to choose from but they all start with your basic block. So, make a master copy of your basic skirt block in card so that it will last and can be repeatedly used to copy from – the copies will then be adjusted to make your new designs.

BASIC SKIRT

Your basic skirt is fairly close-fitting, with darts in the front and back for shape around the waist and a slight kick at the hemline; it will be the shape you have toiled and finalized, but you may want to consider changing the length...

Lengthening your basic skirt

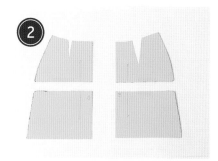

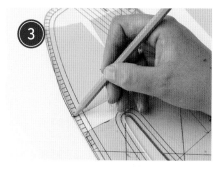

1 The simplest way to lengthen your skirt is to add to your hemline. However, this may widen the skirt at the bottom more than you want. Alternatively, you can cut your pattern at the hipline...

2 ...and add your additional length at this point, making sure the adjustments are the same on the front and back pattern pieces.

3 Take your tailor's curve and redraw the gap between the pieces: this way the fit and the length are changed but the hemline shape is unaltered.

Shortening your basic skirt

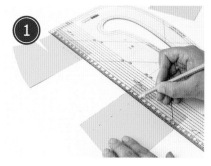

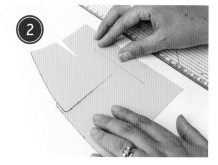

1 To shorten the skirt without affecting the shape of the hemline, cut across at the hipline. Calculate how much you want to remove; measure and mark across the lower part of the pattern at this point.

2 Overlap your pattern pieces. Double-check that your pieces are correctly matched and that your grainline still matches, then tape them together.

3 Smooth the curve of the side seam using your tailor's curve and trim away any excess at the join. Repeat the steps for the back block.

PENCIL SKIRT

You can create a more slimline shape by removing the 'kick' at the hem.

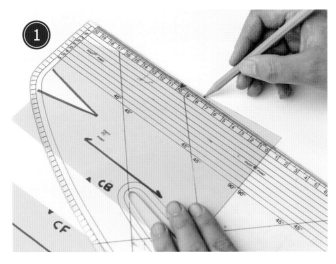

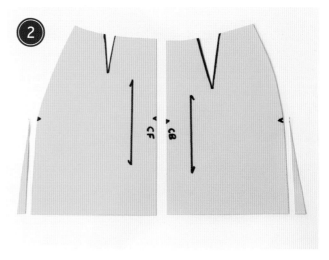

1 Simply use your tailor's curve to straighten up the side seam. Starting at the hipline, 'square down' until you reach the hem. You want to create a 90-degree angle where the side seam meets the hemline.

2 Cut the excess off and use it to replicate the shape on the other pattern piece. Make sure that both front and back pieces have been adjusted.

Top tip
You may want to consider adding a back vent to a pencil skirt, so that you can move more easily (see pages 78–79).

A-LINE SKIRT

The A-line is a great skirt shape; both casual and practical, it will suit most, if not all, body types, and is one of my wardrobe staples. It fits well at the waist and is shaped over the hips, but also gives you plenty of room to walk, dance and cycle.

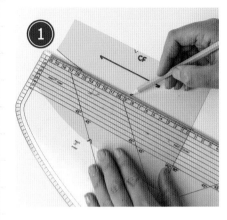

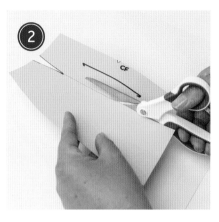

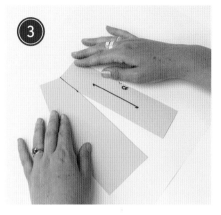

1 Taking your front skirt block, draw a line starting at the bottom of the dart down to the hem, making sure the line is at a right angle to the hemline.

2 Cut along this line but leave a small section of card still attached below the dart.

3 Close the dart by bringing the two sides together. This will create an upside-down 'V' shape in the body of the skirt.

SKIRT SHAPES

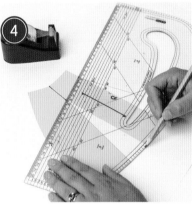

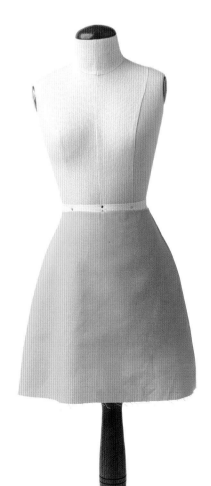

4 Tape the dart together to hold it in place. Using a separate piece of paper, fill in the gap, then smooth the hemline with your tailor's curve.

5 Repeat the same process with your skirt back pattern, as shown.

FLARED SKIRT

Want a skirt with more swish but don't want to lose the fit around the waist?
This is the skirt for you.

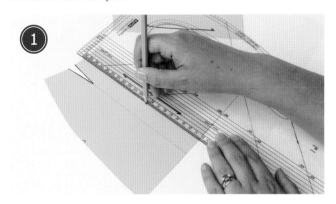

1 Taking the front skirt block, draw a line starting at the bottom of the dart down to the hem, making sure the line is at a right angle to the hemline. Measure and mark a line that is parallel to your centre front (CF), and 4cm (1½in) away from it.

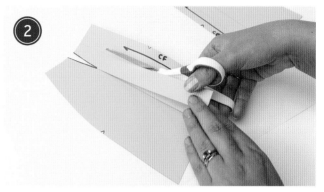

2 Cut along the lines but stop a small distance from both the bottom of the dart and the waistline.

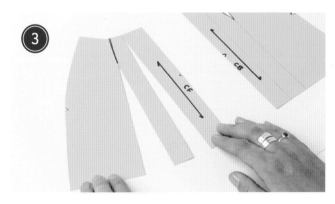

3 Close the dart by bringing the card together, creating an upside-down 'V' shape in the body of the skirt. Tape the dart together to hold it in place. Pivot the CF to create another 'V' in the body of the skirt. You can make this as small as you like.

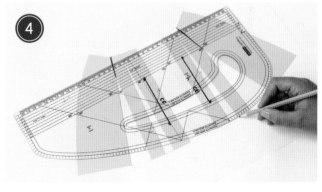

4 Using a separate piece of paper, fill the gaps and then smooth the hemline with your tailor's curve. Repeat the process with the back pieces, as shown.

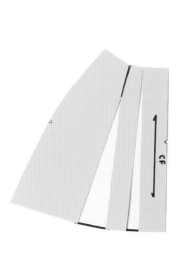

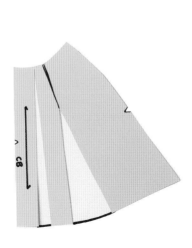

BOX-PLEATED SKIRTS

A box pleat is a great way to add drama, detail and shape to a skirt. Box pleats can be added into the front or back of the skirt and in different positions by either adjusting the block or separating the block and then creating an additional pattern piece, to give you a contrast box pleat.

Version 1: using the dart positions

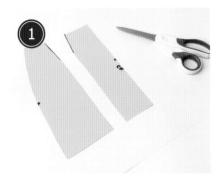
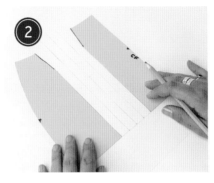
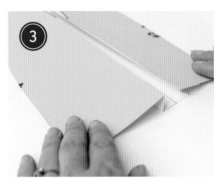

1 Taking your front skirt block, draw a line starting at the bottom of the dart down to the hem, making sure the line is at a right angle to the hemline. Cut along this line and separate the two pieces – the space between them is where your pleat will form.

2 The size of the box pleat is your choice; I would suggest a good size is around 16cm (6in) of additional fabric. With a separate piece of paper, fill the gap and secure with tape. Draw three equally spaced lines between the pieces, creating four equal 4cm (1½in) sections.

3 Fold the paper along the right- and left-hand lines – this will bring the original block back together and shows you how your fabric will behave.

4 Mark the top and bottom of the pleat lines, and the end of the dart position by creating or drawing notches – this will help construction of the box pleat later. (See opposite for how to create a box pleat in fabric.)

This skirt has box pleats inserted at the darts, but with a contrast fabric used (see page 46).

Version 2: using the centre-front position

As with version 1, opposite, you will be adjusting the block to add in your box pleat, but this time we are adding it to the central position. Whether adding this box pleat to the front or back, remember to place the centre position of the new pattern along the fold of the fabric when cutting out.

As with version 1, opposite,

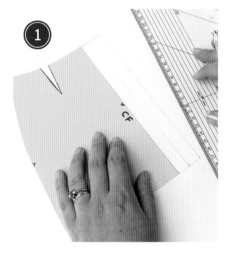

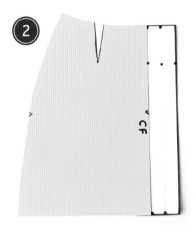

1 Using the centre front of your block pattern as your new box-pleat stitch line, secure a separate piece of paper along the full length of the centre front. Mark out half of your box pleat width along the entire length of the stitch line. For example, if you are using 16cm (6in), of extra fabric, you only need to mark out 8cm (3in).

2 Square up to create a new centre-front line. Trim any excess paper away. Mark the top and bottom of the pleat as well as along the pleat fold lines by creating notches – this will help with construction later.

Constructing your box pleat

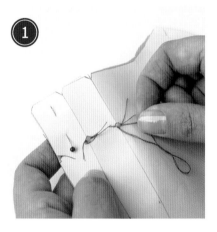

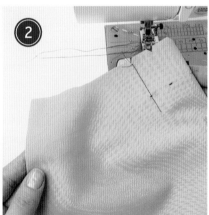

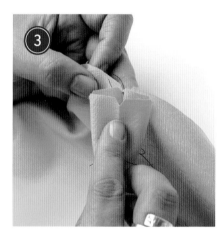

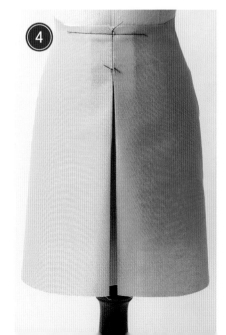

1 Cut your skirt pattern from fabric, then mark the position and size of the box pleat using the notches in your paper pattern, with either tailor's tacks or chalk.

2 Fold the right sides of the fabric together using the centre front as your guide. With the fold on the right-hand side, ensure all notches match before using the left-hand notch as a guide to sew in your pleat. Stitch down about 5cm (2in), or the length of the dart for version 1, finishing with a backstitch to secure.

3 Bring your stitch line and centre fold together, opening out the fabric and pressing to create the box-pleat shape.

4 Secure the top of the pleat with tacking/basting stitches within the seam allowance. Press again. Let the fabric fully cool before removing the tacking/basting stitches.

Constructing your box pleat with contrast fabric

Why not use contrast fabric for your box pleat, so that when you walk your box pleat reveals a flash of colour? To do this, you will need to create a separate pattern for your box pleat. Therefore, draft out your block pattern as normal and create a separate pattern piece that is the full width of your desired box pleat and the full length of your skirt – remembering that when you place your pattern onto fabric you will need to add allowances to all sides of the pattern (seam allowances and hem allowance).

For contrast box pleats at the darts (see page 44)

As on page 44, take the front skirt block, find the centre of the dart and draw a line down from here to the hemline. Cut along this line, to give you two front sections.

Now, draw out a new pattern piece that is the length of your skirt by the desired width of the pleat – let's say 16cm (6in), as before. Measure and mark this into four equal strips of 4cm (1½in). Mark the positions of the darts with notches. Note on the new pattern piece that you need to add seam allowances to the right- and left-hand edges and an allowance at the hem. Also note on your main pattern pieces that you need to add seam allowances to each side of the cut dart line.

For a contrast pleat at the centre (see page 45)

In this example (shown below), you will need to make a note on your skirt pattern that you need to add a seam allowance to what is currently the centre-front line, as you won't be placing this pattern piece on the fold.

Now, draw out a new pattern piece that is the length of your skirt by the desired width of the pleat – let's say 16cm (6in), as before. Measure and mark this into four equal strips of 4cm (1½in). Mark the positions of the darts with notches. Note on the new pattern piece that you need to add seam allowances to the right- and left-hand edges and an allowance at the hem.

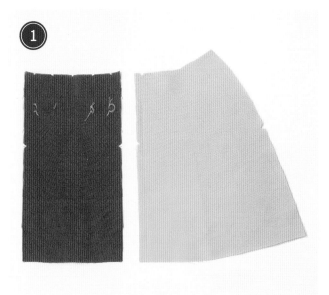

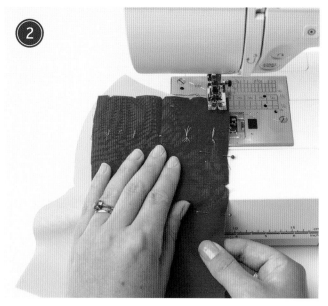

1 Cut out your skirt pieces and contrast box pleat. The number of skirt and box pleat pattern pieces will depend on if you are inserting the box pleat into the darts or central position. Remember to ensure you have added the seam allowances to the relevant areas. Mark the position of the box-pleat fold lines using tailor's tacks or chalk.

2 With right sides together, pin and stitch one side of your box-pleat fabric to your skirt. Then repeat on the other side.

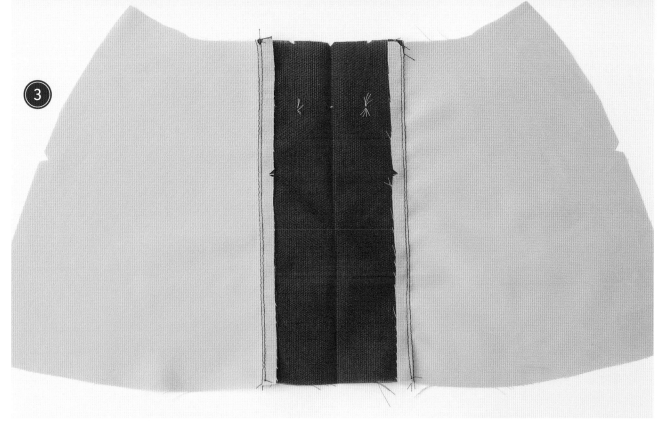

3 Press and understitch your seam allowances towards your box pleat fabric (see page 59).

4 Fold the whole panel of fabric right sides together, using the centre notches as your guide. With the fold on the right-hand side, ensure all notches match before using the left-hand notch (where the pleat fabric joins the skirt fabric) as a guide to sew in your pleat. Stitch down about 5cm (2in) or the length of the dart, if the dart is where you are inserting the box pleat.

5 Bring your stitch line and centre fold together, then open out the fabric and press to create the box-pleat shape (see step 3 on page 45).

6 Secure the top of the pleat with a tacking/basting stitch within the seam allowance to finish.

Top tip

For a more tailored pleat, use a tacking/basting stitch along the full length of the pleat. Press and allow to cool before removing the tacking/basting stitches – this will give you a super-crisp box pleat.

GATHERED SKIRTS

A gathered skirt doesn't necessarily need a block pattern. It can be made very simply out of two rectangles of fabric using two measurements: the desired length of your skirt and half your hip measurement + 23cm (9in), or more depending on how much gather you want. But if you want to add gathers into specific sections of your skirt, you will need to use your block pattern.

Version 1: gathered in the body

Creating a gathered detail in the body of the skirt can make a dramatic statement, especially when using asymmetric lines. For this example, I'm adding a gathered flounce detail from the lower hip to the hem but keeping the waist to hipline intact; but you can draw any shape you want, as the below principles will be the same.

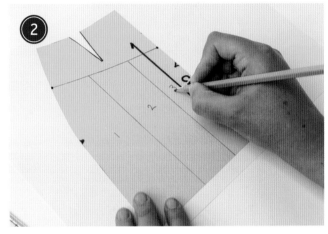

1 Create a line that starts at the side seam and continues to the centre front. As I want to close the dart and create a yoke (see page 72), I have gone below the dart with my line.

2 Divide the lower skirt into several sections – I find three is a good number of sections here. From the hemline, carefully square up to your marked positions, creating sections and labelling them as shown.

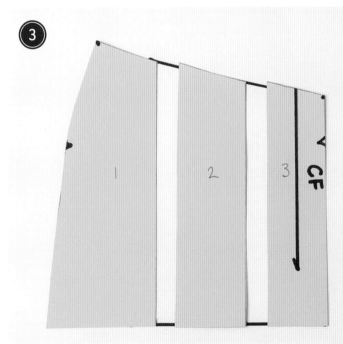

3 Cut away the top section. Add in your extra fabric: I would recommend around 4–5cm (1½–2in) in each section. Repeat for the back-pattern pieces; the shape doesn't have to be the same as the front, but make sure it matches up on the side seams. This is where your side seam notches will help you. This skirt is shown on page 51.

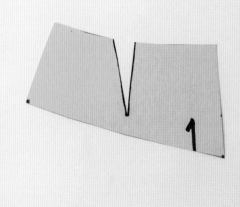

Version 2: gathered at the waistline

You can add gathered detail at the waistline without affecting the hemline by pivoting the card – this gives you a tulip-shaped skirt. If you want a gathered waistline and a fuller skirt, simply separate the pieces by same distance at the waistline and the hemline (see Judy, page 116).

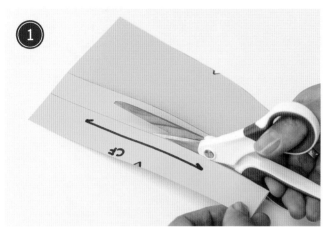

1 Take your front block pattern. Draw a line starting at the bottom of the dart down to the hemline, making sure the line is at a right angle to the hem. Draw another line about 4cm (1½in) to the right, parallel to your centre front. Cut along these lines, leaving a small section of card still attached at the hemline.

2 Open the sections, by separating them at the waistline by approximately 4cm (1½in). This will create 'V' shapes in the body of the skirt.

3 Use a separate piece of paper to fill in the gaps and secure with tape. Reshape the waistline and trim the excess paper away. The dart positions are no longer applicable on your new pattern, but make a note that this is a gathered seam. Repeat for the back pattern piece.

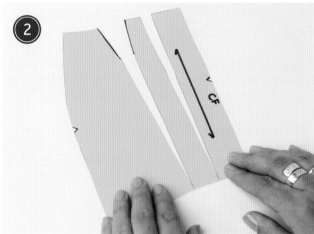

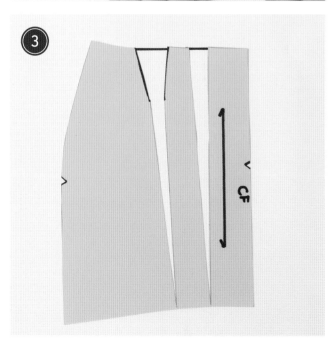

Version 3: gathered tiers

This version is similar to version 1 (on page 48), but this time we are adding several tiers to the skirt. Here, I have already closed the dart to create a yoke (see page 72).

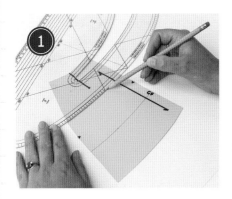

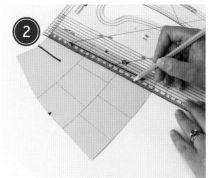

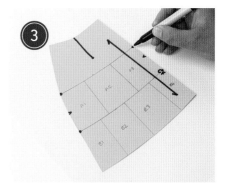

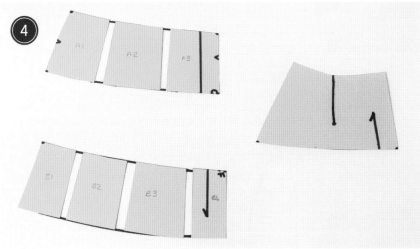

> ## Top tip
> Remember to make notches and pattern notes clear when adding to or adjusting patterns. It really will make it so much easier when you come to stitch your skirt together.

1 If you are wanting to lengthen or shorten the skirt, make sure you do this step first. Using your tailor's curve, create two or three tiers in the length of the skirt, ensuring that the tiers match at the front and back side seams of both pattern pieces.

2 Divide each tier into panels, and with each new tier add an extra section each time.

3 Number each piece ready to be cut into sections. For example, A1, A2, A3, then B1, B2 and so on for the second tier. Also add notches at the side seam and centre positions where the sections meet.

4 Place a separate piece of paper underneath your pattern sections, then begin to open out each section equally to create a new pattern. The distance you separate the sections will determine how much gather you are adding to the skirt. I would recommend around 5–7cm (2–2¾in) in between each section.

5 To bring the skirt back together, simply gather the upper seam of the second tier, match the notches to the first tier/yoke (see opposite for sewing in gathers) and stitch together. Then repeat by gathering the third tier's upper seam and matching the notches with the lower seam of the second tier and so on. Repeat with the back pattern piece.

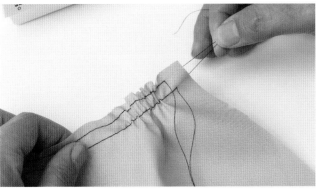

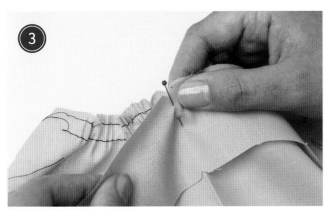

How to sew in gathers

Whichever gathering option you decide (see pages 48–50), the way you sew in your gathers will be the same.

1 Along the seam allowance that is going to be gathered, sew two lines of parallel stitching with an extended stitch length. The first line needs to be within the 1.5cm (⅝in) seam allowance, for instance, 1cm (⅜in) away from the raw edge; the second line needs to be outside the seam allowance, for instance 2cm (¾in) from the raw edge. This will give you a channel.

> ### Top tip
>
> Before sewing the two lines of parallel stitching, change your bobbin thread to a different colour as this will make it easier to identify which thread is which later. Pulling the bobbin thread is a lot easier that pulling the top thread.

2 Pull both of the bobbin threads to start to create a gather. You may want to do this from both side seams, rather than trying to gather the whole skirt from one side.

3 Match up your notches and side seams to the notches on the other fabric pattern piece, before distributing the gathers so that they align and fall evenly along the seam. Then, with a normal straight stitch, secure the seam in place before removing the temporary gathering stitches and pressing the seam.

FASTENINGS & FIXTURES

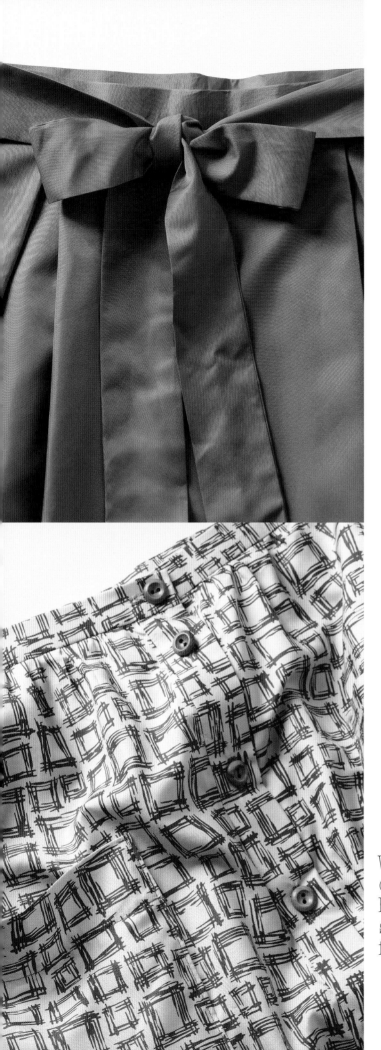

When thinking about your design, and before cutting any fabric, you will need to consider how you are going to get in and out of your skirt. This section gives you several options, from ties and zips to buttons, depending on the style you want.

TRADITIONAL WAISTBAND

The traditional waistband is suitable for all styles of skirts, whether they have pleats, gathers or darts, or if the skirt opens at the front, side or centre back. It is a quick way of finishing off the raw top edge professionally. The waistband is normally one of the last details to be added and may or may not come with a tab. Here, I have used it on a skirt with a centre-back seam. I always use interfacing to add body to the waistband by fusing or tacking/basting it to the wrong side of the fabric before construction. Interfacing gives structure and will stop the waistband from rolling or creasing.

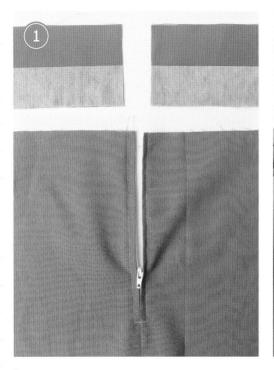

1 Before we draw out your waistband, we need to check your toile for your garment's waistband measurement. With the tape measure, measure around the toile's waistline – this takes into account all the seams, darts and details that affect the waistline, as these are already sewn in place. However, you will need to extend the length: to accommodate a button placket add 6cm (2½in); for a tab add 3cm (1¼in), as I've done here. (See also the tip box, below, for a faster cutting and measuring option.)

Draw a rectangle using the new waistband measurement as the length, and double the width you want your finished band to be. When using this pattern piece, remember to add your 1.5cm (⅝in) seam allowances to all sides, and to place your pattern piece so that the length of the waistband follows the fabric grain. For the interfacing, cut out the same pattern length, but half the width, and adhere to the wrong side of your fabric, as shown above.

2 Place the raw edge of the waistband to the waistline raw edge. Pin in place, ensuring that you have left your seam allowances free. Here, my tab allowance is overhanging the centre-back edge.

Top tip

For a speedy sew, cut a strip about 15cm (6in) longer than your natural waist measurement – we will trim off the excess later.

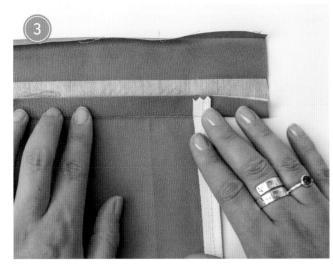

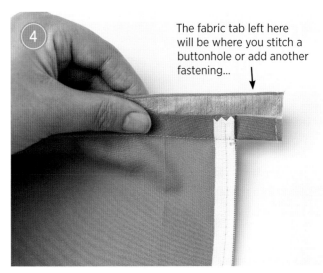

The fabric tab left here will be where you stitch a buttonhole or add another fastening...

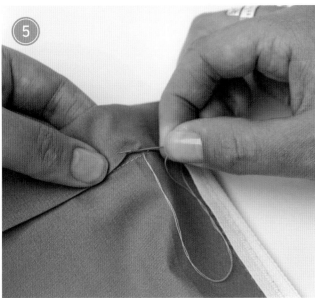

3 Stitch the waistband to the waistline, taking a 1.5cm (⅝in) seam allowance. Press this seam allowance into the waistband and prepare the opposite side of the waistband by pressing the seam allowance along the length.

4 Turn the waistband back on itself with the right sides together. Pin and stitch at both ends of the waistband, ensuring that the seam allowances are turned up. Note: be mindful of your fixtures, as the seam allowances may vary here, especially if you are adding a fastener or a button placket. If you are using the speedy solution (see tip box, opposite), you will need to trim the waistband to size before stitching.

5 Clip the corner seam allowances and turn out the waistband, making sure the corners are nice and crisp. Hand-stitch the waistband to the garment using ladder stitch. Add your chosen fixture, such as a hook-and-eye, button and buttonhole or snap fastening to finish.

WRAPPED WAISTBAND

To create a wrapped skirt, all you need to do is double up a pattern piece. For instance, if your skirt wraps in the front (see Grace on page 124) then you will need two front skirt pattern pieces: one to attach to the back-left side seam and one to attach to the back-right side seam. The vertical seams on the two front skirt patterns will need to be finished with a hem. To create a waistband for a wrapped skirt, you need to make the traditional waistband a lot longer, so that you can tie it in a bow, and add a buttonhole at the side seam to feed the tie through. Before adding your wrapped waistband, make sure your back skirt is attached to the two front skirt pieces, and that you have created a hem on both the right- and left-hand front vertical seams of your skirt (see pages 80–83 for different hem finishes).

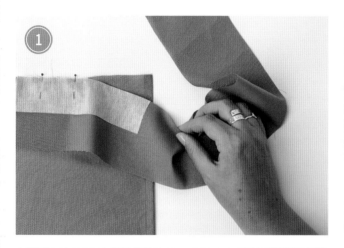

Finish here, just before you get to the skirt...

Start here...

1 To create your wrapped waistband pattern, you will need to multiply your natural waist measurement by three – this will become the length of your waistband and will be long enough to wrap around your waist and tie a modest bow. The width of the finished waistband will need to be doubled for the pattern. Depending on the full length of the waistband, you may need to halve the pattern and cut out two pattern pieces, which will need to be stitched back together again later; therefore, be mindful when it comes to adding your seam allowances. Cut out your fabric using your pattern, remembering to add seam allowances to all sides before cutting out. The interfacing will need to be half the width of your pattern and only needs to be approximately the length of your skirt's waistline. If your waistband has a join, match the waistband seam to the skirt's left side seam first, and use this positioning to attach the interfacing at the correct place along the waistband. Fuse the interfacing in place before pinning the waistband to the skirt, right sides together.

2 Secure the waistband in place with a straight stitch and a 1.5cm (⅝in) seam allowance. Press the seam upwards along the skirt top.

3 Fold the length of the waistband back on itself, with the right sides together and pin in place. Starting at one folded edge of the waistband, sew together, pivoting at the corner, and continuing along the waistband until you almost meet where the skirt is attached (the annotations, left, should help you). Clip away the bulk at the corner, then repeat on the other side of the wrap.

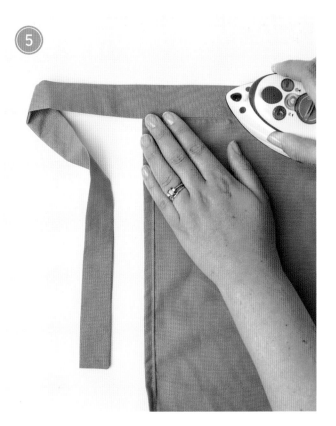

4 Turn through, making sure the tips of the corners are nice and crisp by using your chopstick to push them out. Repeat on the other side.

5 With the whole waistband turned through, pin the remaining waistband in place with the seam allowance tucked under, and press. Secure the length of the waistband in place by either topstitching on your machine or by hand-sewing in place with ladder stitch.

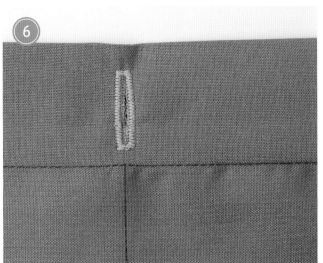

6 Now you need to create an opening for your waistband so it can wrap around your waist. Sew a buttonhole in your waistband, on the right-hand side, in line with your side seam. It must be big enough for your waistband to pass through.

FACING

When dealing with skirts, a facing is an invisible waistband that is sewn into the inside of a garment. It provides a clean-edge finish and also covers the raw edges, giving a smooth and comfortable waistline. It is perfect for use with back or side zip fixtures for a clean and sleek finish. The facing, like the waistband, is one of the last details to be added to a garment.

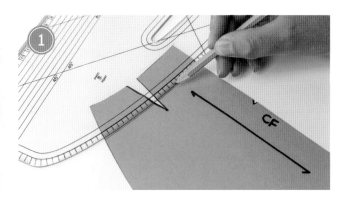

1 Make a pattern for the facing by using the top 5cm (2in) of your skirt's pattern (see above, left). Any darts or details that affect the waistline shape will need to be closed (see above, right) before creating a pattern. Depending on where your fixtures are positioned, you may have two or three pattern pieces. Remember to add seam allowances to all sides and create a notch at the centre points of both the skirt waistline and facing.

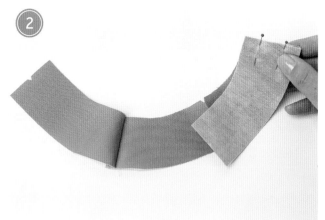

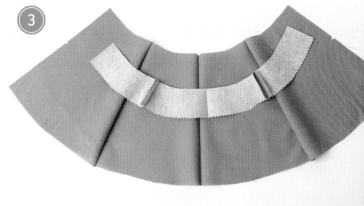

2 Cut out the fabric using the pattern and interface the wrong side of the fabric. Sew the facing pieces together to create a facing band.

3 Press the seams of the facing band open. Finish the longer edge of the facing with pinking shears, or a zigzag or overlocking stitch. Before aligning the facing with the skirt, make sure all details that affect the skirt's waistline, such as darts and pleats, have been completed.

4 With the right sides together, line up the seams and raw edges.

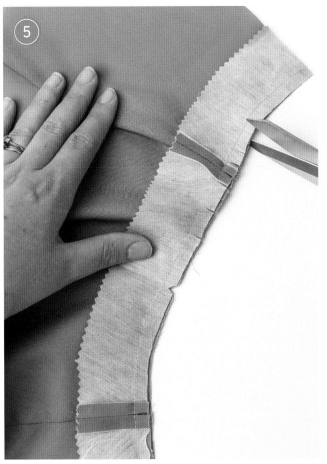

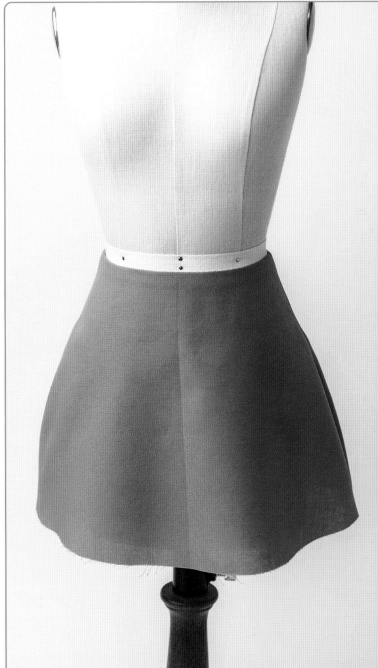

5 Pin and stitch together with a 1.5cm (⅝in) seam allowance. Snip into the seam allowance to remove any excess bulk and to allow the seam to sit smoothly when the facing is pressed over to the inside.

6 Understitch the seam allowance to the facing, close to the stitch line. This will give a clean finish and stop the facing from rolling to the outside (see also box below).

7 Turn the facing to the wrong side of the skirt. Press in place and then hand finish by turning under and stitching the seam allowance by the zip opening and also stitching the facing to the side seams of the skirt to anchor it down.

Top tip

To understitch the facing, press the seam allowances onto the facing. Keeping the main skirt pieces clear, stitch 3–6mm (⅛–¼in) from the seam, securing the seam allowances to the facing.

ZIP FASTENINGS

Zips are a great way of fastening and securing garments. There are many types of zip, and the look and finish you are after will determine which option you choose. Your zip will need to be stitched to your garment before adding a waistline finish like a waistband or facing.

Centred zip

This method is a great technique for beginners. As the zip teeth are positioned in the centre of the seam, it's a simple way of partially hiding the teeth of the zip, giving you a clean finish. It's ideal for a back-seam fastening, as shown in this example.

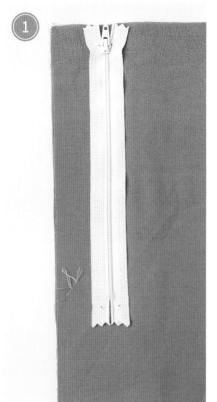

1 In order to add a zip into your skirt you need to add a seam allowance to your back-skirt block, along the centre-back position. Therefore, your back-skirt pattern will need to be two pieces rather than one whole pattern piece. Simply remember to add a 1.5cm (⅝in) seam allowance to the centre-back position and don't place the pattern on the fold when cutting out your fabric.

To insert your zip, first mark out where your zip finishes by placing the zip at the top of the waistline's raw edge, making sure the zip teeth start 1.5cm (⅝in) down from the top raw edge. Then follow the zip tape along the centre-back seam. Mark where the zip teeth finish.

2 Pin the two back pieces with the right sides together. Extend the stitch length to the longest length and sew the seam, from the top down, with a 1.5cm (⅝in) seam allowance until you get to the marked zip end position. This line of stitching is a temporary tacking/basting stitch. Keep the needle in the fabric while you adjust your stitch length back to a normal length. Backstitch before continuing to complete the seam.

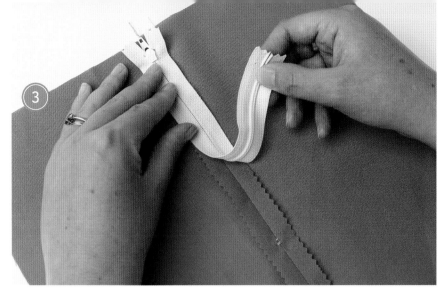

3 Press the seam open, then finish the raw edges by pinking or overlocking them. With the wrong side of the fabric facing up, place your zip face down with the teeth over the seam. Pin it in place.

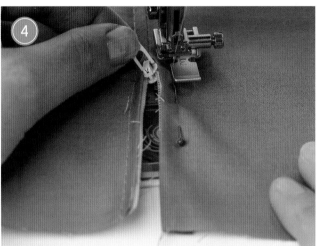

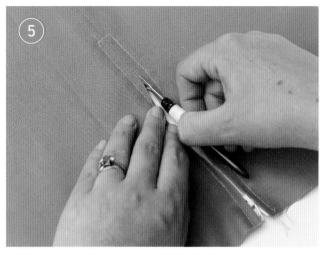

4 Turn the fabric over, so you are now looking at the right side. Before stitching in place, I would suggest inserting new pins that are accessible from the top, or tacking/basting the zip in place with a running stitch and then removing the pins. Unpick about 5cm (2in) of the tacked/basted seam, starting at the top raw edge. This will allow you to move the zipper head up and down.

Change your standard foot to a zipper foot. Starting at the bottom of the zip and at the seam line, topstitch the zip in place by sewing across the zip tape to the right and then pivoting to stitch parallel to the seam line. When you are close to the zipper head, leave the needle in the fabric and lift the presser foot. Unzip, so the zip head passes under the zipper foot before lowering the presser foot to continue the topstitch. This process should prevent a kink in your topstitching as you sew around the zip head. Adjust your zipper foot and repeat on the other side.

5 Remove the remaining tacking/basting stitches and press.

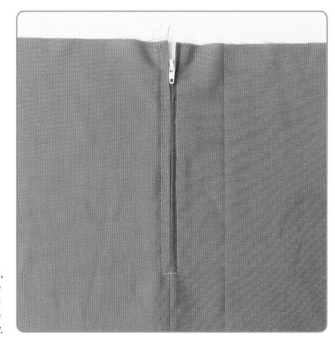

There are other zip finishes, such as lapped or invisible zips, so do your research if you want to include anything more complicated. Remember though, that as you are creating your skirt from scratch, you will need to adjust your base pattern to add seam allowances accordingly.

Fly zip

This finish is perfect for skirts. A fly zip is normally found on a pair of jeans, so you will be familiar with it even if you have not sewn one before. It gives a really nice finish as well as detail to the garment and completely hides the teeth of the zip. Just be aware of how you attach the zip. I use this little mnemonic: 'girls are always right, so boys are left'. Sorry boys. It means that the right-hand side of the garment should be on top of the left-hand side for girls, and vice versa. So now you know why shirts, blouses, coats, waistbands etc., fasten differently for boys and girls, as the rule applies there, too.

Top tip

Make sure you use the right size zip for this type of zip finish, and ensure your zip end mark really is away from the end, to ensure there are no broken needles. My suggested metal zip size would be 15cm (6in).

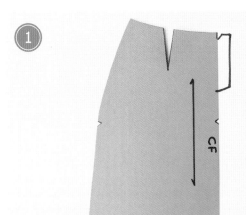

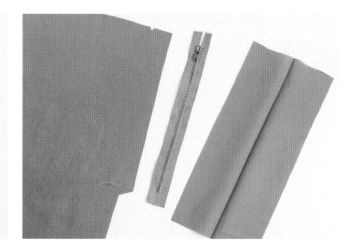

1 Because you will be putting a seam along the centre front, your skirt front will need to be two pieces rather one whole pattern piece (and your back piece can be just one). You will also need to adjust your pattern to accommodate the fly front. To do this, measure and mark out the length of the zip teeth, along the centre-front line – this is especially important when using a metal-toothed zip! From the waistline to the marked position, create a 'tab' along the centre-front line that is 1.5cm (⅝in) wide. Create a notch where the centre front meets the waistline and angle the bottom of the tab at the marked position, so that it will be a more comfortable finish; when cutting out, remember to add seam allowances along the whole centre front as well as the rest of the pattern. Do not place this pattern on the fold. To create the zip facing, or guard, cut a separate pattern piece that is approximately 12cm (4¾in) wide and slightly longer than your zip length.

2 Cut two pieces of fabric for the skirt front (and cut your skirt back). Before removing the pattern pieces, transfer all the notches onto the fabric. I like to double-check the notch against the end of the zip teeth at this stage, to prevent any broken needles. Place the front pieces right sides together and add a tailor's tack to mark the bottom of the zip teeth.

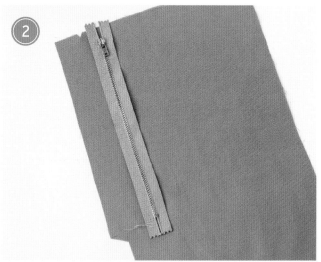

3 Extend the stitch length to the longest length on your machine, to give yourself a tacking/basting stitch. Starting at the centre-front notch, stitch down to the marked zip end position, leave the needle in the fabric, then adjust the stitch length back to normal. Backstitch before finishing the rest of the seam.

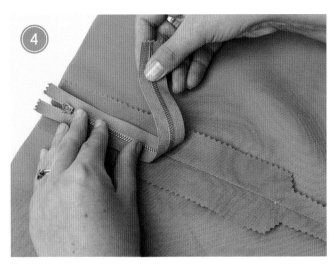

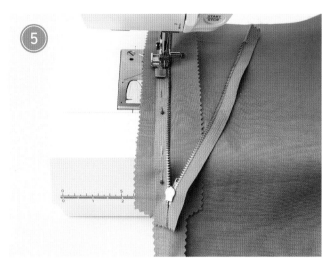

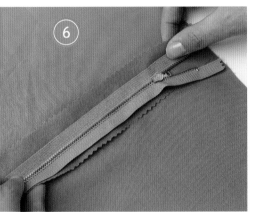

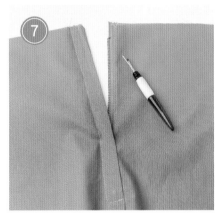

4 Lightly press the seam open, then pink or overlock the raw edges of the seam allowance. Place the right side of the zip face down, with the teeth along the centre of the seam, making sure the top of the zip teeth are not in the waistline seam allowance.

5 Pin the left side of the zip tape to the left side seam allowance. Change your standard foot to a zipper foot, then stitch the left-hand side of the zip in place, sewing approximately 6mm (¼in) from the zip teeth.

6 Pull the right-hand side of the zip tape to the edge of the right-hand seam allowance and pin through all the layers. Turn the fabric over and pin or tack/baste to secure, ready to topstitch in place.

7 To ensure that you catch the zip tape as you topstitch, I would mark out the stitching line with chalk or a water-erasable pen – across the bottom of the zip and up the side. Starting at the base of the zip, sew along your stitch line towards the waistline. Remove any tacking/basting stitches.

8 Taking your zip facing piece, fold in half lengthwise, with the right sides together. Sew along the length and the bottom width of the fabric towards the fold to create a guard. Trim the seam allowance, turn out and press.

9 Pin and the stitch the guard to the to the left-hand seam allowance only. This gives you a really clean finish.

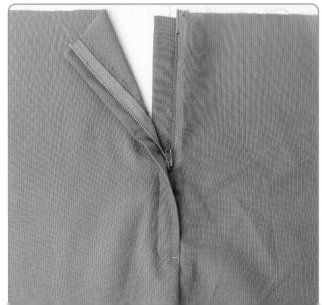

BUTTON PLACKET

A placket is an opening at the neck or sleeve of a garment, or in this case, a way of getting in and out of your skirt, while adding a design feature. The placket will provide support and strength to the garment's fastening, as the placket will consist of two layers of fabric as well as a layer of interfacing, which will then house the buttons and buttonholes.

Similarly to the fly zip, be aware that the placket will overlap in the front – the right placket will need to overlap the left one; you will need to add the placket to the skirt before adding the waistband finishes.

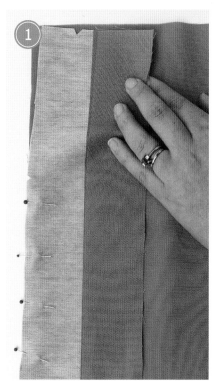

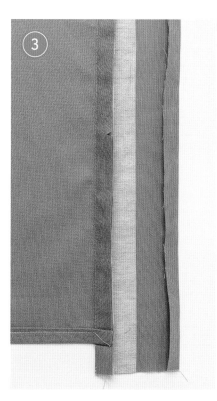

1 To add a button placket, your front skirt pattern will need to be two pieces rather than one whole pattern piece (and the back will be one whole piece). However, as we are adding a separate placket piece you will not need to add a seam allowance to the centre-front line, as the placket pattern is designed to extend beyond that point.

To create the pattern, your placket needs to match the length of your finished skirt, so you do not need to account for any hem allowances. The width of the finished placket is your choice, but here I have gone for a 3cm (1¼in) finish. However, my pattern piece needs to be 6cm (2½in) in width, as I'm folding my placket piece rather than creating a contrasting one (see Cecilia, page 100). Before cutting out your two fabric plackets you will need to mark the centre-front position of the placket with a notch. To do this, measure 1.5cm (⅝in) (as this is half of your finished 3cm/1¼in width) from the left-hand side and mark the top of the pattern (this is now your left-hand side placket) and draw your grainline parallel to the length of the placket. Then remember to add your 1.5cm (⅝in) seam allowance to all edges. To cut out the right-hand side placket, simply flip the pattern or cut the pattern out while the fabric is folded with right sides together – you will use the centre-front notch to position your buttonholes and buttons later.

For your interfacing, cut out the same length but only half the width, twice: one for the left and one for the right. Fuse to the wrong side of the placket on the side with the notch. With the right sides together, pin the right placket to the right-hand skirt front, along the centre-front seam.

2 Stitch in place from the top down, until you get to the hemline (the hem fold line, not the raw edge). Press the raw seams towards the placket and trim the seam allowance. Press under a 1.5cm (⅝in) seam allowance on the other placket edge – fold the placket back on itself so that the raw edges are contained. At the waistline, tack/baste the placket together. Repeat to this point on the left-hand placket. You will need to pause the placket construction here and complete other steps like the waistline finishes and, possibly, the hem finishes before returning to complete the placket.

3 Complete your waistline and hem finishes. For this example, I have sewn a double hem (see page 82) but you can tuck these out the way, if you prefer, to leave the hem until later. Either way, you need to be able to see the placket seam allowances overhanging.

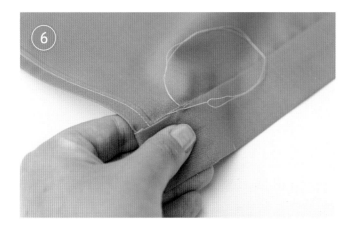

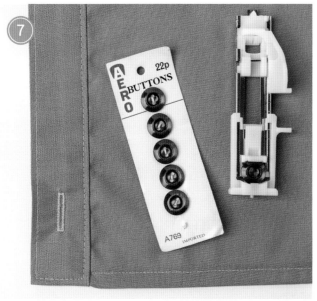

4 Fold the placket back on itself, so that the right sides are together (if you didn't hem your skirt at step 3, tuck the hem allowance out of the way and into the skirt).

5 Stitch across the width of the placket, at the hemline, making sure the remaining placket seam allowance is also folded back on itself, as shown.

6 Trim and remove the bulk before turning the placket back the right way. Poke out the corner and ensure all the seam allowance is enclosed within the placket before pinning and pressing. Hand-stitch the placket closed, close to the original stitch line.

7 Topstitch in place along the placket edges to give a detailed finish, using a contrasting thread. Repeat with the left-hand placket before adding buttonholes and buttons to finish.

Top tip

The spacing and number of buttons is down to you, but use the centre-front notch to get the correct position. A sewing gauge will also help to accurately space your buttonholes and buttons quickly.

Taking it further

For a contrast finish on your placket, you will need to carry out these few steps before following the above instructions:

1. Follow the drafting instructions in step 1, but this time adjust your placket pattern width to 3cm (1¼in). This doesn't include seam allowances – these will need to be added to all sides – and it doesn't affect the positioning of the centre-front placket notch. You will now need to cut two of everything – two from main fabric, two from lining fabric and two from interfacing. If your fabric is folded with right sides together, you only need to cut once to get right- and left-hand side pieces. Fuse the interfacing to the wrong side of the main fabric pieces.

2. Stitch one of the main fabric pieces to one of the lining pieces, right sides together, along the length of the placket. Repeat with the other two fabric pieces, making a second set that is a mirror image of the first.

3. Continue by pinning the pieces to the skirt fronts, with the main fabrics right sides together. Then follow the rest of the instructions from step 2 onwards.

DETAILS & FINISHINGS

Make your skirt truly unique by adding little details and finishing touches such as pockets, hems and a back vent.

PATCH POCKETS

I love a pocket! In my opinion, no garment is complete without one. Not only are they functional, they are a great way of adding detail and decoration to your skirt – think contrasting lining or topstitched details, for example. From patch pockets to inseam pockets and yoke pockets, the choice is yours!

Lined patch pockets

The patch pocket is the simplest pocket to create as you do not need to alter your pattern block to accommodate it. You simply attach the pocket to the right side of the fabric and secure it in place with topstitching. Where the pocket goes – on the front, side or back of the skirt – is up to you.

Top tip

If you are placing two matching pockets on your skirt, I would suggest marking on the block pattern where you want them to go with notches. This will help to ensure symmetry on either side of the skirt.

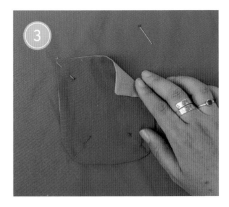

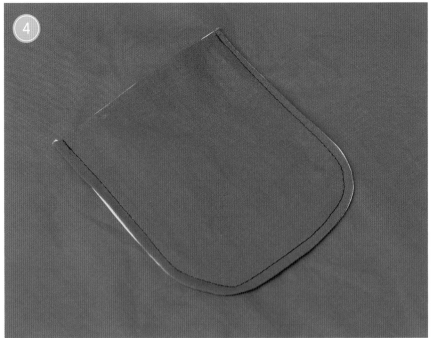

DETAILS & FINISHINGS

1 The shape and size of the pocket is up to you, but I would suggest making a pattern piece so that you can ensure that each pocket is even and the right shape before you cut your fabric. Add 1.5cm (⅝in) to all sides of the shape, then cut one from main fabric and one from lining fabric.

2 With the right sides together, pin, then stitch around all the sides with a 1.5cm (⅝in) seam allowance, leaving a gap of about 4cm (1½in) in the middle of a straight seam (the gap can be at the side or bottom, but must not be on the top seam. This way the topstitching later secures the gap firmly). Clip the corners and remove any excess bulk from the seams.

3 Turn the pocket through, poke out the corners, then press. Hand-stitch the gap closed, before placing the pocket in position on the skirt. With the lining of the pocket on the right side of the skirt fabric, pin in place.

4 Secure the pocket with a topstitch. Finish the top corners of the pocket with backstitch.

Top tip

To give additional strength and detail to the corners of the pocket opening, stitch a box or triangle rather than using backstitch to secure the pocket corners.

Unlined patch pocket

Like your lined patch pocket, the shape and size of these pockets is your choice, but you should create a pattern so that you can ensure that the pocket is even and the right shape before you cut your fabric. Once you have the finished shape drawn out, you will need to add a different set of seam allowances compared to your lined patch pocket (see step 1 instructions, below).

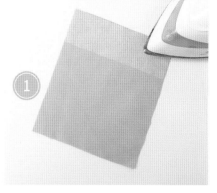

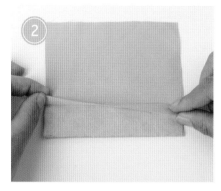

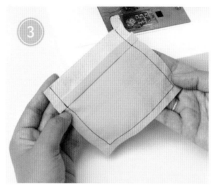

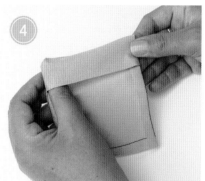

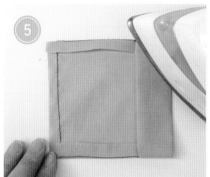

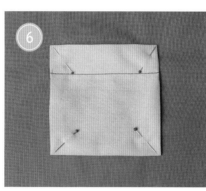

69

Top tip

Whether your pocket has a square or curved bottom, stitch around the pocket with an extended straight stitch and a 1.5cm (⅝in) seam allowance at step 3. This will give you a guide as to where to press under the raw edges in steps 4–5.

If your pocket has a curved bottom, gently pull the bobbin thread of your extended stitch to ease the curved shape when pressing.

1 Take your pocket pattern and add 5cm (2in) to the area that will be the pocket opening (usually the top of the pattern, but not always) to create a hem; also add your normal 1.5cm (⅝in) seam allowances to all sides. Make notches along the seams at the 5cm (2in) and 1.5cm (⅝in) positions before cutting out your fabric. I like to add a bit of interfacing to the hem allowance of the pocket as it gives a little bit of structure and strength to the area. Fuse interfacing to the wrong side of the pocket hem.

2 Press over the hem at the 5cm (2in) notches with the right sides together. Then, leaving this fold in place, fold and press the 1.5cm (⅝in) seam allowance over with the wrong sides together, as shown. Pin in place.

3 Secure your folds by sewing them in place with a 1.5cm (⅝in) seam allowance and ending with backstitch. Then, with an extended stitch length, continue around the remaining edges of the pocket using the same 1.5cm (⅝in) seam allowance (see tip box, right).

4 Turn out your top hem. Using the extended stitch lines as your guide, turn under the seam allowances. Your stitches should sit on the very edge of the fold.

5 Press the folds. Your sewn lines should sit on the very edge of each fabric fold.

6 Secure the hem by topstitching or hand-stitching. Place the wrong side of the pocket onto the right side of the skirt fabric, in the position you want it. Pin it in place.

7 Topstitch the pocket in place. Finish the top corners of the pocket with backstitch (see tip box opposite for extra finishing details).

INSEAM POCKET

The great thing about an inseam pocket is that it looks incredibly professional, but you don't need to adapt your block pattern to fit one! You can add one into either a side seam or where the yoke meets your skirt... basically if there is a seam, you can add a pocket to it! The inseam pocket is meant to be a discreet and clean-finished pocket, but that doesn't mean you can't use a bright coloured or patterned fabric to add a little peak-a-boo touch!

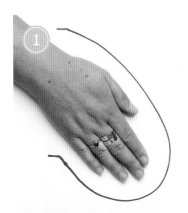

1 The quickest way to create your inseam pocket pattern is to draw around your hand. You will need to be mindful of where your pocket is going, as you will need to follow the shape of the seam you are inserting the pocket into; also, the way your hand will move in and out of the pocket may determine the shape. For this example, I'm inserting the pockets into the side seams of the skirt, therefore the angle of my hand and wrist is determining the shape of the pocket and the pocket's opening seam. Remember to add seam allowances to the pattern's edges as well as making a notch on both the pocket and skirt pattern pieces, so you know where you want your pockets to be attached to the skirt before cutting them from fabric.

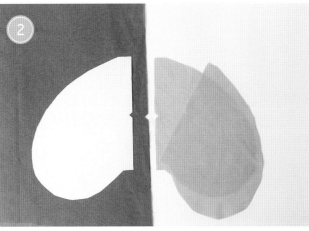

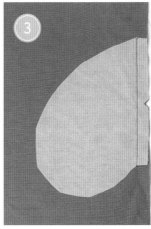

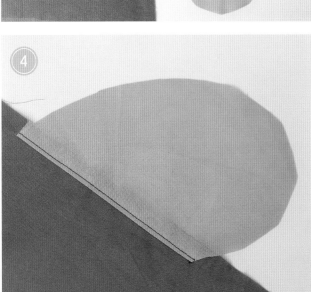

2 Using your pocket pattern, cut out your fabric: you will need two pieces that are a mirror image of each other. The easiest way to ensure this is to fold your fabric so that the right sides are together, and then just cut your pattern out once for a pocket pair. Repeat to create another pocket for the other side of the skirt, if you are having two pockets.

3 Taking one of the pocket pairs, place one of the pocket pieces onto the right side of the skirt front, right sides together; align the notches and pin in place. Repeat with the other pocket piece, this time with the right side of the back skirt, right sides together. Secure with a straight stitch taking a slightly narrower than usual seam allowance. If you are adding another pocket to the left-hand seam of the skirt, repeat this step again with the other pocket pair.

4 Press open the pocket and then understitch the pocket to the seam allowances – this will stop your pocket lining from sticking out (see page 59). Repeat with all other pocket pieces.

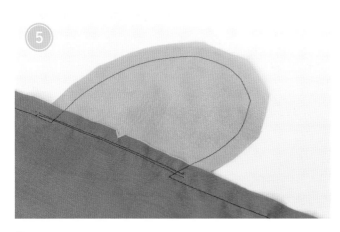

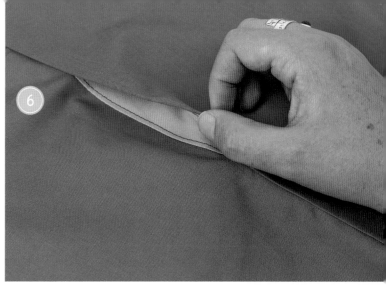

5 With right sides together, pin and sew your seams together as normal, however, this time you will need to divert your stitch line to go around the pocket. To do this, make sure you leave your needle down when pivoting the fabric to get to the pocket's seam allowances. You will need to do this at the top and bottom of the pocket opening, before continuing along the remainder of the seam.

6 Once you have pressed and finished your seams, your inseam pocket will be neatly contained within the seam, and only visible when you move your hands in and out of the pocket.

YOKE

A yoke is a great way of adding shape and detail to a garment. It is a separate and shaped pattern piece that is positioned along the waistline and tends to have a clean finish, so no darts are present within the pattern piece. The yoke will then be reattached to the remaining skirt pattern and can be applied to the front or back of a skirt only, or to both! You can also add further details to the yoke by adding piping or an opening for a pocket. A yoke can be straight or shaped (below you can see the blocks for both). Whatever shape you choose, you will need to adapt your block. As the yoke is positioned at the waistline, it can be finished with a waistband, or a lining that will be the same shape as the yoke.

Top tip

You can add further details to your skirt if you wish, like piping or pockets onto the yoke. You may even wish to add detail to the lower part of the skirt by adding flare or a box pleat.

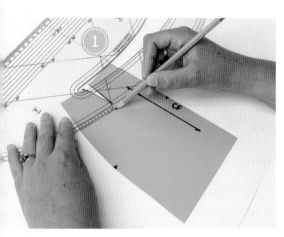

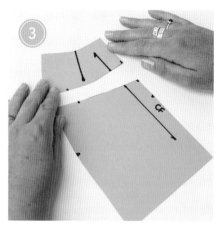

1 For this example I'm adapting the front skirt block only. Use your tailor's curve to draw in your yoke shape – the shape you create is up to you, however, if you are creating a yoke for the front and back of the skirt, make sure the yokes meet at the same point on the side seams.

2 Draw a series of notches along the yoke line – the centre position is an important one, not to be missed. This will make it easier to sew the pieces together later. Also ensure that the grainline is extended into the yoke section.

3 Cut along the yoke line to separate the lower skirt. If your block has a dart like this one, close the dart and smooth out any uneven areas with your tailor's curve or by hand. If your yoke goes part way through the length of the dart, this is not a problem. Simply close the yoke's dart for this step. The remaining dart in the skirt will either be stitched in place, as for Pattie on page 96, or you can alter the remaining skirt shape by closing the dart or adding a detail like a box pleat.

4 Before cutting out your fabric, remember to add seam allowances to your pattern, especially to the edge where you have added the notches, otherwise your skirt will not match your yoke. For a continuous yoke, place the centre position on the fold and do not add seam allowances to that edge. Transfer all notches to the fabric before removing the pattern.

5 Reconstruct the skirt by attaching the yoke to the skirt bottom. Pin in place, with right sides together, ensuring that the notches match, before stitching.

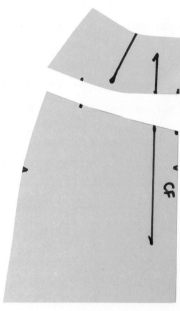

A straight yoke.

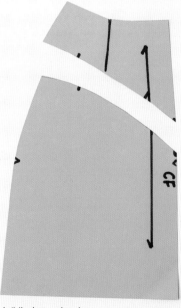

A 'V'-shaped yoke.

DETAILS & FINISHINGS

Sewing a neat, 'V'-shaped yoke

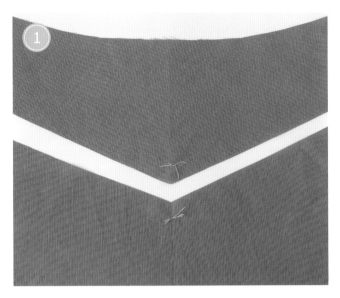

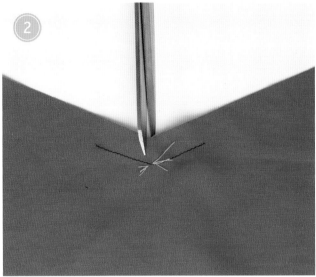

1 Cut out your skirt and yoke pieces from fabric and mark the position of your centre notches with tailor's tacks.

2 You will need to make a small clip into the point of the 'V' on the lower skirt piece. First sew a line of stay stitching, using a 1.5cm (⅝in) seam allowance, along the 'V' section of the lower skirt (this prevents the fabric from distorting). Clip into the 'V', making sure that you do not cut the stay stitching. This allows the fabric to open up or close down when you come to stitching this pattern piece to the yoke.

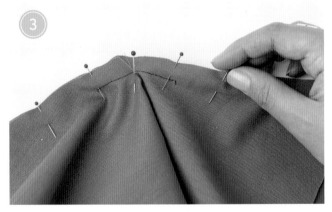

3 Pin the yoke and skirt front together, carefully easing the fabric around the 'V', then stitch and press to finish.

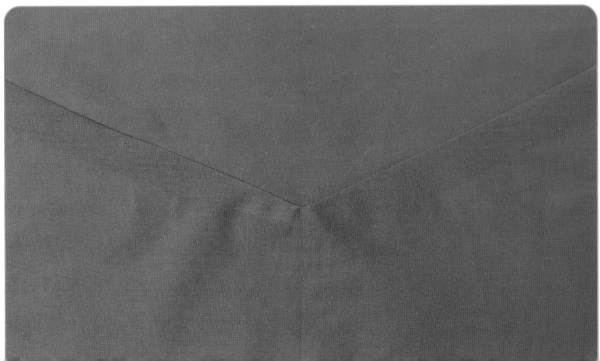

YOKE POCKET

A yoke pocket is sewn into the side seams and waistline of a garment and the opening can be curved or at an angle. You will be familiar with yoke pockets as they tend to be a regular feature on trousers and jeans. The yoke pocket can look a little complicated at first glance, but with a little pattern adjustment, it will be totally worth it for the finished look.

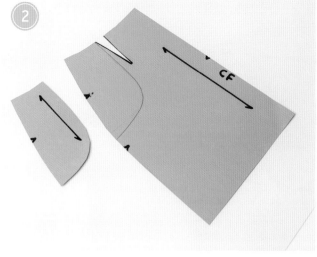

1 Taking your front block pattern, draw a curve from the waistline to the side seam, making sure you don't affect the dart position. You may want to place your hand there to get a gauge of how big you want your pocket to be. The whole of this shape will be the pocket yoke.

2 Trace this shape off the block to create the pattern piece. Also create notches and transfer the grainline so that the pieces can be lined up later.

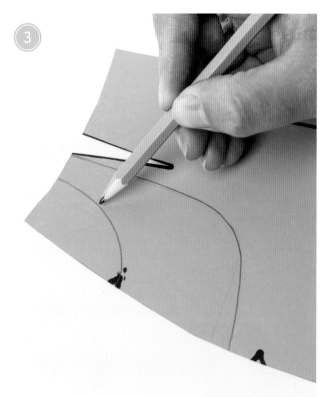

3 On the block, draw a line for the pocket opening. This can be at an angle or curved. Try to leave a good distance from where the pocket yoke meets the side seam and waistline, but bear in mind that it needs to be big enough for you to get your hand in and out. Trace this shape off the block to create your pocket lining pattern piece. Again, create and transfer notches and the grainline.

4 You should have two separate pocket pattern pieces in addition to your skirt block pattern now. Adjust your skirt pattern by cutting along the pocket opening line you created in step 3 before adding seam allowances to all pattern pieces.

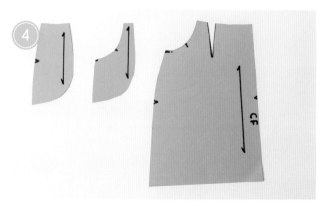

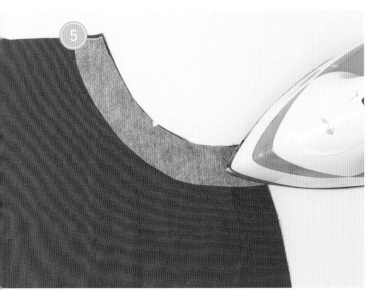

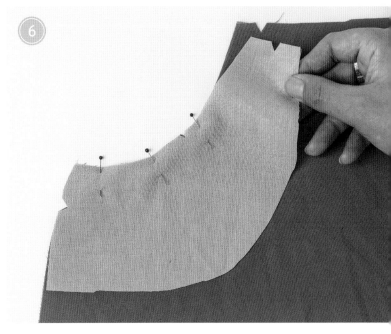

5 Cut out your fabric: the skirt and pocket yoke should be cut from the main fabric and the pocket lining should be cut from lining fabric. Whether your pocket opening is cut on an angle or is a curved shape, you will need to support and prevent that area from over-stretching because of the bias. Fuse interfacing to the wrong side of your front skirt pattern's pocket opening.

6 With the right sides together, pin your pocket lining to your skirt front piece, matching the notches at the side seams and the waistline.

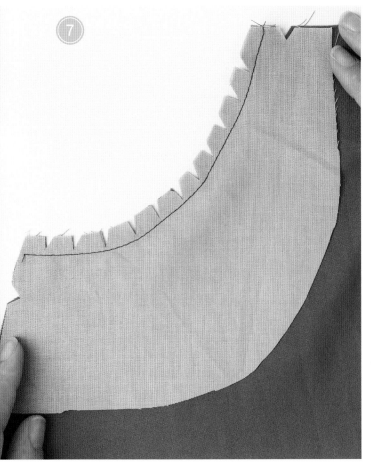

7 Stitch your pocket lining in place using a 1.5cm (⅝in) seam allowance. Clip or trim the seam allowances to reduce bulk.

8 Turn the pocket lining to the wrong side of the skirt and press, before understitching or topstitching in place (see page 59).

continued overleaf

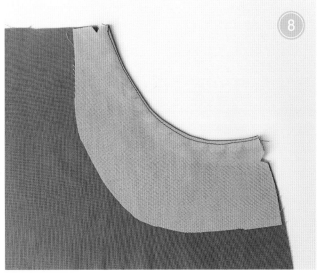

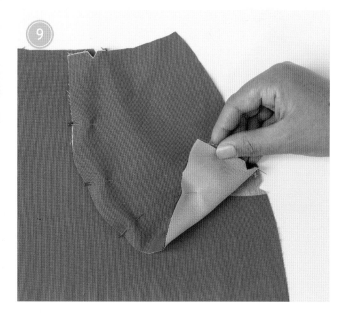

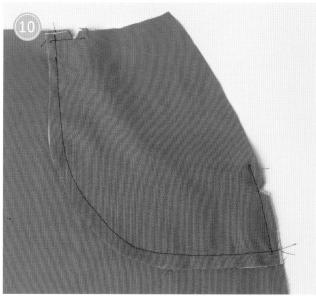

9 Place the pocket yoke right sides together with the pocket lining and pin. Place it on the wrong side of the skirt front piece, lining facing down, making sure the side seam and waistlines match up. Make sure you are only handling the pocket yoke and lining, not the skirt front.

10 Stitch the pocket pieces together around the bottom/inner edge, being careful not to catch the skirt front. Press and finish the seams. Then, through all layers, and using a stay stitch within the seam allowance, sew where the top of the pocket meets the waistband, and where the side of the pocket meets the side seam. You can see it from the wrong side, above...

11 ...and from the right side, below. This will help keep the pocket in place when you sew the side seams together as normal.

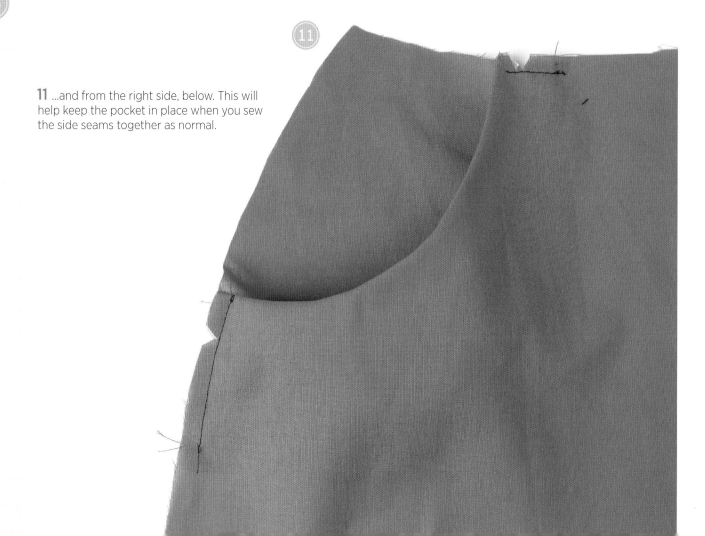

For further details on this feature
pocket, see Kate on page 108.

BACK VENT

A back vent is a vertical opening that starts at the hem of a skirt; the opening happens along the back seam to allow for ease of moment. When making a slim-fitting skirt (such as Monroe on page 88), you may want to add a back vent so that you are able to walk more easily.

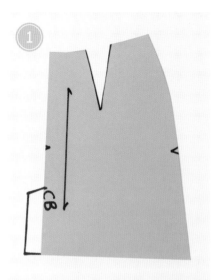

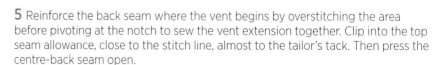

1 To add a back vent pattern, all you need to do is create an oversized seam allowance along the centre-back position. Taking the back skirt block, measure 27cm (10½in) up from the hemline along the centre-back position and create a notch. From this notch, square out by 5cm (2in). Repeat this step at the hemline and join the points of reference up and angle the top, to create the vent extension (the angle will make a more comfortable finish). Before cutting out the pattern, remember to add your seam and hem allowances, ensuring that a seam allowance is added to the centre-back line and around the vent.

2 Cut out and transfer all the notches to the fabric, making sure you have transferred the notch at the top of the vent with a tailor's tack.

3 Before sewing the back seam and any fixtures that affect the back seam, you will need to finish the long edges of the vent extension. You can do this by finishing the raw edge with a double hem – turn under and press the edge of the fabric twice by approximately 1cm (⅜in) each time, then sew the seam to secure it.

4 Place your skirt back pieces right sides together. Complete any back-seam fixtures before pinning and stitching the back seam together. Sew down to the tailor's tack. Backstitch at this point before extending the stitch length and continuing down towards the hemline – this tacking/basting stitch will give you a clean crisp vent when pressing the skirt later.

5 Reinforce the back seam where the vent begins by overstitching the area before pivoting at the notch to sew the vent extension together. Clip into the top seam allowance, close to the stitch line, almost to the tailor's tack. Then press the centre-back seam open.

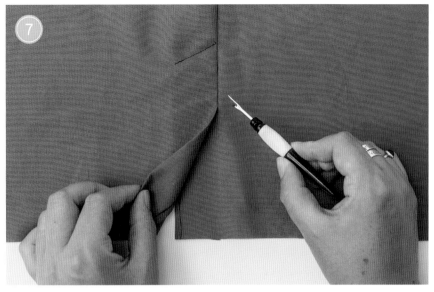

6 Finish the seam before opening out the fabric and pressing the vent extension to the left back side (the right side if you are looking at the wrong side of the fabric).

7 Turn the fabric over, then topstitch the top part of the vent extension to the left back side of the skirt. This will keep the vent in position. Remove the tacking/basting stitch from the vent. Continue with the rest of the skirt construction and then hem the skirt to finish.

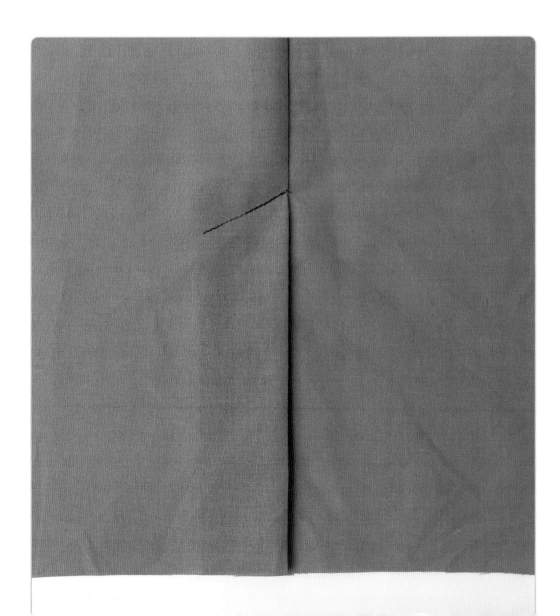

HEMS

The hem is normally the last detail to be completed on a garment, and it is a way of finishing off the raw edge of a skirt so that it does not fray. You could hem your skirt with a simple finish or use it as an opportunity to add a sprinkle of detail.

Bound hem finish

This is one of my favourite ways to finish my skirt hems. By using a contrasting fabric to create the bound hem, you can add a pop of colour and a super clean and stylish finish to your skirt. The bound finish can be used on a straight or curved hemline – all you need to do is use bias binding (you can make your own or buy ready-made). Before cutting your fabric out, you will need to add a 1.5cm (⅝in) seam allowance to your hemline.

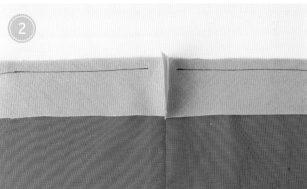

1 Whether you want your binding to be seen (finish 1) or unseen on the right side (finish 2), a good width of bias strip would be 6cm (2½in) (seam allowances are included in this measurement), giving you a 1.5cm (⅝in) binding on finish 1 or a 3cm (1¼in) binding on finish 2. Cut out your bias strips. Place the right side of the binding to the right side of the skirt hem, raw edge to raw edge. Start at one of the side seams, leaving enough fabric overhanging for a seam (you will pin the other end of the strip to this at the end, making sure the join lines up with the skirt side seam). Pin in place.

2 Secure in place with a straight stitch, making sure you leave a gap of about 2.5cm (1in) before and after the skirt side seam, ready for the next step.

3 Bring the excess binding together to create a join. Match up the join with the skirt's side seam and mark with a pin. Sew the binding together where the pin is positioned, then trim off any excess fabric. Press the binding seam open.

4 Finish stitching the binding to the skirt hemline.

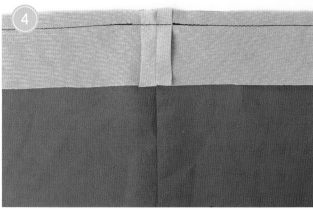

Bound finish 1

This first option allows you to enclose the raw edge with the binding as you would with a quilt, so that the bias binding is visible from the right side. Simply fold the binding raw edge to meet the raw edge of the fabric and press. Fold the binding over itself again to hide your first line of stitching. Secure in place with a hand-stitch, or machine finish by topstitching or 'stitching in the ditch'.

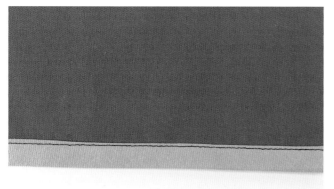

Topstitching along the edge of the binding.

Stitching along the very edge of the binding, 'in the ditch'.

Bound finish 2

The alternative is to press the seam allowances to the binding, before turning the binding to the wrong side of the skirt, much like a facing. Topstitch in place, creating a neat single line of stitching on the front and a bound finish on the inside of the skirt. Alternatively, hand-stitch in place. This is a great finish for a more curve-edged skirt, or if you wanted to add a bit of structure to the edge of the skirt. Another idea is to press more of the main fabric hem up as shown on page 83.

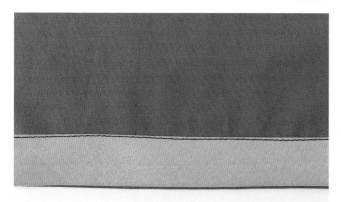

The bound facing on the wrong side of the skirt.

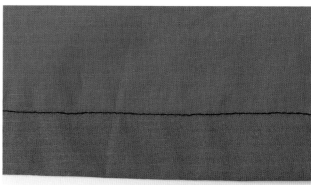

The topstitched hem visible on the right side of the skirt.

Double hem

A double folded hem is an enclosed seam – the raw edges are concealed, giving you a neat finish. How deep you have the hem will depend on the shape of the hemline. If your skirt has a relatively straight or flat hem then a deep hem can be used. If the hem is curved, a narrow hem will be required otherwise unwanted folds and pleats will occur in the fabric. Before you even cut out your fabric, make sure you add enough hem allowance to the hemline of your skirt pattern. It needs to be twice the depth you want, as you will be turning it back on itself twice.

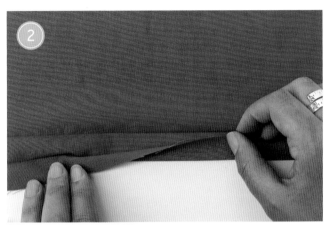

1 With the wrong sides together, fold the raw edge to the finished hem level you want. Pin and press in place along the circumference of the hem.

2 Remove the pins before folding the hem into itself again, so that the raw edge is along the pressed line. Pin in place and press again.

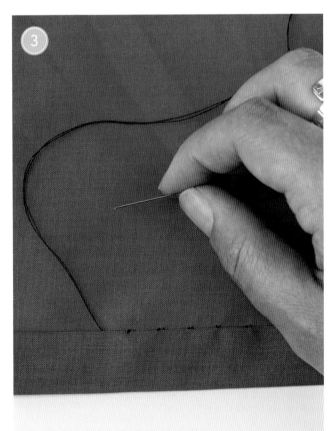

3 To finish, either hand-stitch the hem (as shown left), or secure with topstitching on your machine (as shown above).

For further details on this
bound hem finish, see
Cecelia on page 100.

PUTTING YOUR SKIRT TOGETHER

Now you have all the skills you need, it's time to choose a design and get sewing! How you assemble your skirt will depend on the details you have chosen, but I have put together a beginner's guide, which may help you along. As with most things, there is always more than one way to make something – so if you find that you are doing things in a different order to me, that doesn't necessarily mean you are doing anything wrong. Do what is easier or right for you! After all, it is your skirt, your way!

SO HERE IS MY SUGGESTED ORDER OF THINGS...

Sewing in details that affect the shape of the skirt, such as pleats and darts, is normally my first job, as I find it is easier to construct and press these details while the fabric is still a single flat piece.

Next in line would be anything that affects the body of the skirt – including details like yokes, or patch or yoke pockets. An exception would be an inseam pocket, as I wouldn't complete the pocket until sewing the side seams together in the next step.

Fixtures and fastenings like zips and button plackets come next – sometimes details like the button placket, aren't finished until later on, but you probably need to start them now in order to get to the next stage.

Next you'll sew the side seams together – I love this stage as you really begin to see your skirt taking shape.

Then comes adding the waistline finish – whether this is a waistband or a facing. Once this is attached you can try the skirt on and work out where your hemline should be.

PUTTING YOUR SKIRT TOGETHER

And finally, it's the hemline to finish – the best bit! Depending on your hem finish, I would normally complete any hand-stitched finishings here as well. This would include linings of the waistband, placket and, of course, hand-stitched hems.

Monroe LOOKING SHARP: PENCIL SKIRT

Not just for the office, the pencil skirt is a wardrobe staple that has never gone out of fashion! Switch up the fabric and you can change something from corporate staple to straight-out sassy! Here I have chosen a classic pinstripe with a contrast facing to add a little personality... perfect for when there is a strict office uniform but you still want to be individual.

Elements used

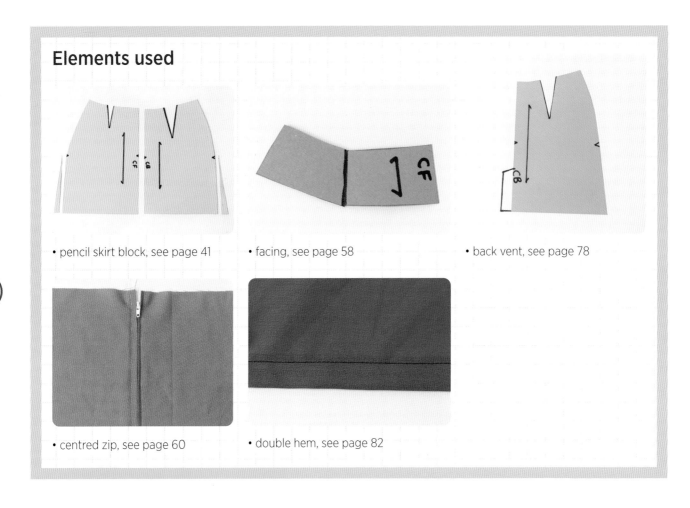

• pencil skirt block, see page 41

• facing, see page 58

• back vent, see page 78

• centred zip, see page 60

• double hem, see page 82

Creating your pattern

1 Adjust your basic skirt block to create a pencil-skirt shape, remembering to adjust both the front and back pattern pieces (see page 41).

2 Create your facing pattern by using the first 5cm (2in) of your basic skirt block, from both the front and back pieces. Close all the dart openings before tracing onto your drafting paper (see pages 58–59).

3 Next you need to add your back-vent allowance to your back-skirt pattern. You can do this directly onto the drafting paper as it is not a separate pattern piece, rather an extension to part of the centre-back seam allowance (see page 78).

4 Add your 1.5cm (⅝in) seam allowances and transfer all notches and grainline details to the paper pattern – note that your skirt front and front facing patterns are to be placed on the fold, so no seam allowance will be added here. Also, as you are double hemming your skirt, I would suggest adding 5cm (2in) in total for the hemline for this shape of skirt (see page 82 for more tips). Cut the pattern pieces out.

5 Position the patterns on your fabric, ensuring the centre-front of the skirt and centre-front facing pattern pieces are on the fold, and the back skirt and back facing pattern pieces are in line with the grainline (see page 20). Pin in place, cut out and transfer the notches onto the fabric.

Making your skirt

1 Sew up the darts in both the front and back skirt pieces (see page 34).

2 Prepare your two back skirt pieces for adding your centred zip and back vent by placing them right sides together, making sure all the notches line up. Pin in place. For ease, you may want to finish the long vertical edges of your back vent now, before adding the zip (see step 3 on page 78).

3 Follow the centred zip instructions to insert the zip (see page 60), remembering to adjust your stitching again at the lower notch, as you are going to be adding a back vent here, rather than continuing the back seam to the hem of the skirt (see step 4, page 78).

4 Next, create your back vent. You may have already completed most of it, by finishing the raw vertical edges of the vent and tacking/basting the remaining back seam. Stitch and press the back vent (see pages 78–79).

5 Bring the front and back skirt pieces right sides together and stitch the side seams in place, then press and finish the seam edges (see page 21).

6 To give your skirt's waistline a clean finish, it is now time to add your facing to your skirt. Interface your facing pieces before sewing the side seams together. Add your facing to the waistline of your skirt by placing the right sides together, matching up the seams and notches, then pin and stitch in place (see pages 58–59).

7 To finish, double hem your skirt (see page 82).

When making a slim-fitting pencil skirt, the back vent is a must-have detail that will also help you move more easily.

A contrast facing is the perfect way to add a little personality to your skirt, as well as giving a clean waistline finish.

Brodie THIS SKIRT IS MADE FOR WALKING!

I was gifted this awesome tweed fabric from Korbond after doing an event to celebrate their new range, which was inspired by the textures of tweed; the geometric floral fabric reminds me of thistles, which I think complements the tweed's texture. This is a great skirt to wear on a walk or to cycle in, as the box pleat gives you that little bit more room to move.

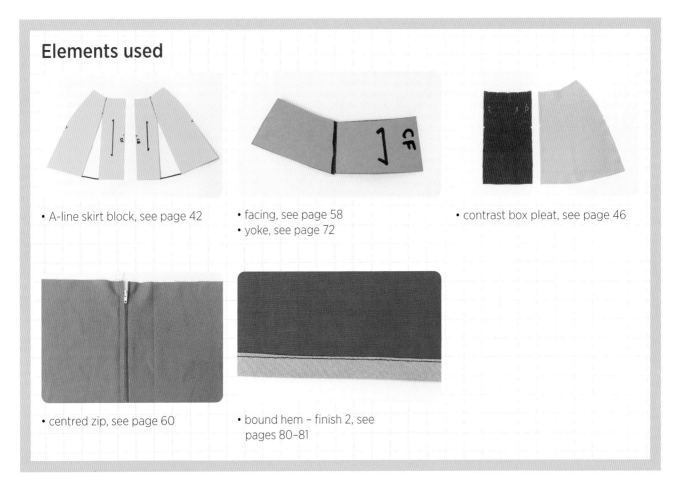

Elements used

- A-line skirt block, see page 42

- facing, see page 58
- yoke, see page 72

- contrast box pleat, see page 46

- centred zip, see page 60

- bound hem – finish 2, see pages 80–81

Creating your pattern

1 Adjust your basic skirt block to create an A-line skirt shape (see page 42), remembering to adjust both the front and back pattern pieces.

2 The shape of yoke is your choice – I decided to go with a clean 5.5cm (2¼in) band that looks like a waistband. Mark out your yoke shape, add notches and cut away from the pattern, giving you two separate front skirt and two back skirt pattern pieces. Note that you will not need to close the dart as you have already done so in the first step.

3 I wanted to add a hook-and-eye fastening on a tab at the back – to do this add about 4cm (1½in) in length to the right-hand back yoke; the construction is similar to the traditional waistband (see page 54).

4 For the facing, you don't need to draft anything else as you are going to use the yoke pattern pieces. So remember to cut these pattern pieces out twice – once in the main fabric (for the yoke) and once in the lining fabric (for the facing), not forgetting the extra tab, which will need to mirror the main fabric, so flip the pattern pieces before you cut the facing.

5 You will need to create a separate pattern piece for the contrast box pleat (see page 46). To calculate the length of the box pleat, you will need to measure the remaining length of your skirt, as you have removed a section for the yoke.

6 Transfer all notches and grainline details to the paper pattern as well as your 1.5cm (⅝in) allowances for both the seams and your bound hem – note, that the only patterns to be placed on the fold are your front yoke and front facing, so no seam allowances will be added here. Cut out the patterns.

7 Position the patterns on your fabric, ensuring the centre-front yoke and centre-front facing pattern pieces are on the fold, and that all remaining pattern pieces are in line with the grainline. Pin in place, cut out and transfer the notches onto the fabric. Here, the box pleat, facings and binding are in a contrast fabric.

Making your skirt

1 Prepare your front skirt pieces for the contrast box pleat (see page 46); stitch and press your box pleat in place. Next add your front yoke to the front skirt, with the right sides together and matching up all notches before stitching (see page 72); you don't need to finish the seam allowances as the facing will enclose them.

2 Place your two back skirt pieces right sides together. Make sure all the notches line up before inserting your centred zip (see page 60). Now you need to add your back yoke pieces to the back of the skirt – place them right sides together, remembering that the back right-hand side has the extended tab for a hook-and-eye, then stitch.

3 With the right sides together, join the front and back skirt pieces, making sure all the seams and notches match. Stitch and finish the seams.

4 Interface your facing pieces before sewing the side seams together. Add your facing to the waistline of your skirt by placing them right sides together. Match up the seams and notches, pin then stitch in place (see page 58). To give a clean finish on the inside, press under a 1.5cm (⅝in) seam allowance on the remaining length of the facing, before hand-stitching this to the seam where the yoke meets the skirt to enclose the seam (similar to the traditional waistband, see page 54).

5 Now for the final sprinkling of detail: your bound hem (see finish 2 on page 81). Your skirt is now ready to ramble!

Bring some colour to your box pleat and hem by using a vibrant contrasting fabric.

Zips and waistline finishes don't need to just be functional... go on – add a pop of colour!

Pattie MOD-STYLE BASICS!

Here, I used the basic skirt block for the overall shape but added a yoke to give
a neat, banded finish at the waistline, like a waistband. I also shortened the skirt
to give it a 1960s-style look, and as I am a *dedicated follower of fashion*,
I decided to top if off with vintage buttons.

Elements used

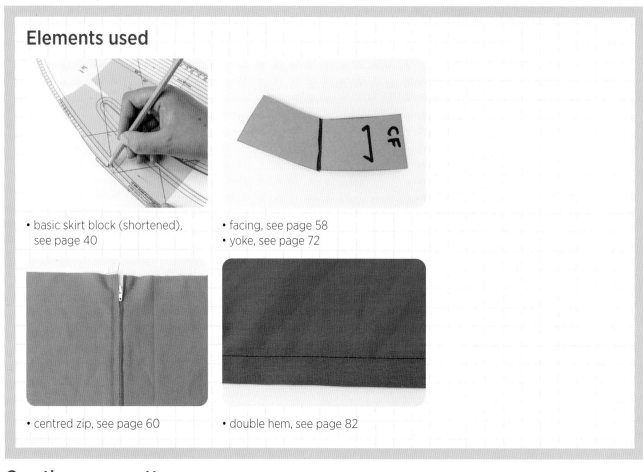

• basic skirt block (shortened),
  see page 40

• facing, see page 58
• yoke, see page 72

• centred zip, see page 60

• double hem, see page 82

Creating your pattern

1 First, shorten your basic skirt block to your preferred
length (see page 40); remember to adjust both the front
and back pattern pieces.

2 Next create the yoke. The shape of yoke is completely up
to you, but I decided to go with a straight band 5cm (2in)
wide. Using your shortened basic skirt pattern; mark out
your yoke shape, add notches, cut away from the pattern,
then close the dart position – giving you two front skirt and
two back skirt pattern pieces (see page 72).

3 For the facing, you don't need to draft anything else as
you are going to use the yoke pattern pieces for this. So,
remember, cut these patterns pieces out twice – once in the
main fabric (for the yoke) and once in the lining fabric (for
the facing).

4 Trace your patterns onto drafting paper and add all your
1.5cm (⅝in) seam allowances as well as transferring all
notches and grainline details to the paper pattern (note, that
your front skirt and front yoke/front facing patterns are to
be placed on the fold, so no seam allowance will be added
here). As you are double hemming your skirt, I would also
suggest adding 3cm (1¼in) in total for the hemline for this
shape of skirt (see page 80 for hemming options).

5 Cut the patterns out and place onto your fabric – ensure
all the pattern pieces relating to the front are on the fold,
and all pattern pieces relating to the back are in line with the
grainline. Pin in place, cut out and transfer the notches onto
the fabric (see page 20).

Making your skirt

1 First, stitch all the darts into place. Then we need to stitch the yokes to the lower skirt pieces – ensure that the notches are matching by pinning them in place before stitching. (For tips on creating a 'V'-shaped front yoke, see page 73.) Do this for both the front and both back pattern pieces but don't worry about finishing the seams as they will be enclosed in the facing.

2 Insert your centred zip into the centre-back seam (see page 60), making sure that where the yoke meets the skirt the seams are pressed towards the waistline, ready for the facing.

3 With your zip in place, it's time to sew the side seams together. Place the front and back pieces right sides together and pin in place, making sure that the yoke pieces are matching at the side seams. Stitch, press, then finish the seams (see page 21).

4 Interface your facing pieces before sewing the side seams together. Add the facing to the skirt by placing it right sides together with the yoke, matching up the seams and notches, then pin and stitch in place (see page 58).

5 Double hem your skirt (see page 82).

6 If you want to be *in with the in crowd*, add buttons to the front of the skirt. Use a sewing gauge or ruler for perfect button spacing.

I like the way the yoked band creates a smooth waistline finish, while the darts add that extra detail in the body of the skirt, framing the button placement.

> ### Top tip
> When facing a yoke, to give a clean finish on the inside, press under the 1.5cm (⅝in) seam allowance on the remaining open seam, before hand-stitching this to where the yoke meets the skirt to enclose the seam.

Understanding your facing will stop it from rolling out at the waistline (see page 59). I have also hand-finished the zip, rather than topstitching it. It's little details like these that will give a clean, crisp finish to your skirt.

Cecelia A CORDUROY CLASSIC

Corduroy is my favourite dressmaking fabric! It has its challenges – working with the nap is a big one – but it's simple if you use a walking foot and keep an eye on the nap when placing pattern pieces. This cute skirt is full of 'coy' little details: the contrast-bound hem, pockets, waistband and placket linings all give little glimpses of colour and pattern.

Elements used

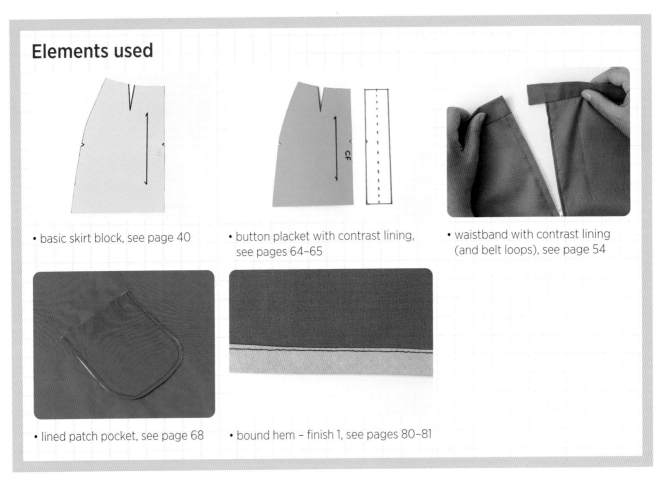

- basic skirt block, see page 40

- button placket with contrast lining, see pages 64–65

- waistband with contrast lining (and belt loops), see page 54

- lined patch pocket, see page 68

- bound hem – finish 1, see pages 80–81

Creating your pattern

1 I was pleased with the shape and length of my basic block for this skirt so I didn't need to make any changes, but of course you can lengthen or shorten if you want to (see page 40). Remember to adjust both front and back pattern pieces if you do.

2 Draw out your button placket pattern – draft this once, but remember to cut out twice so you have a placket for both the left- and right-hand sides of the skirt (see page 64). I created a contrast finish, so that the back of the placket is different to the front. To do this, adjust the placket pattern width by half (you will cut an outer and lining piece for both plackets, then sew them back together – see taking it further box on page 65).

3 For my waistband length, I used my toile's waistline measurement plus 6cm (2½in) to give me extra to cover the button placket (see page 54). As I wanted to add belt loops to my waistband, I needed to create a waistband with a lining, which will be sewn together, rather than a single pattern piece which is folded, so adjust the waistband pattern width by half.

4 For the belt loops, I cut a strip of fabric 6cm (2½in) wide – this will give you a finished width of 2cm (¾in) given that the seam allowance is 1cm (½in). The length of the fabric strip will depend on how many loops you want and the width of your waistband. If your fabric is particularly thick, you may want to consider adjusting the pattern size to accommodate a lining fabric – your main and lining fabrics would need to be 4cm (1½in) wide to give you the same 2cm (¾in) finish.

5 To create your lined patch pockets, I recommend creating a pattern. The shape is your choice but use the same pattern for both pockets and mark out where you want it on the front skirt pattern to ensure they will be symmetrical (see page 68).

6 Transfer all notches and grainline details to the paper pattern as well as your 1.5cm (⅝in) seam allowances. Note, that the back-skirt pattern is to be placed on the fold, and as you are adding a placket, you therefore do not need to add seam allowances to either the centre-back or centre-front. Also, as you are binding and creating a single hem, I would suggest adding 3cm (1¼in) in total at the hemline (see page 80).

7 Position the patterns on your fabric, remembering that only the back-skirt pattern is to be placed on the fold. Pin in place, cut out and transfer the notches to the fabric. Remember that the half-width plackets and waistband, and the pocket pieces need to be cut from both outer and contrast fabric; the binding is also cut from contrast fabric. Remember that the length of the waistband needs to follow the grainline of the fabric.

Making your skirt

1 Stitch the darts into place on both front and back skirt pieces.

2 Construct your lined patched pockets (see page 68). Attach the finished pockets to the skirt fronts at the notched positions.

3 Prepare your button plackets by interfacing and then attaching the contrast linings, right sides facing. Pin and stitch the plackets to your front skirt's centre-front seams, remembering to stop where your hemline will sit (see page 64). Press the seam allowances under, so they can be stitched to the centre fronts of both front skirt pieces at a later stage.

4 With the right sides together, stitch the front and back skirt pieces together, making sure all seams and notches match. Finish the seams.

5 To make your belt loops, with the right sides together, fold the strip in half along the length of the fabric and stitch together taking a 1cm (½in) seam allowance (if you are using a lining fabric, simply place the main and lining fabrics right sides together and stitch along both long sides using the same 1cm (½in) seam allowance). Trim back the seam allowances before turning out, then press and topstitch.

6 Interface your waistband piece. When you sew your waistband and lining together you will trap one end of your belt loops in place, so position them along the length of the waistband, right sides facing, pin, then sew right sides together with the waistband lining along one long edge. Open out. Then sew the waistband to the skirt top, right sides facing, trapping the other end of the loops in place as you do so. Make sure the tops of the plackets are folded and seams are enclosed before stitching in place. Be mindful of the seam allowances here as well, as you want a clean finish, not an extra 'tab' of fabric (see page 54).

7 To finish off the contrast details, add your contrast binding to your hemline raw edge. I have taken it a step further by creating a bound finish (page 81, option 1) with a single hem by pressing under 2cm (¾in) before hand-stitching the binding in place.

8 Finish off your button placket (see page 65) by enclosing all the raw edges. To finish, mark out and stitch your buttonholes and buttons to the placket and waistband. Note that the waistband buttonhole is always horizontal, while those on the placket can be vertical.

My favourite thing to do is add a contrast fabric to areas like the waistband, placket and pockets. We all have fabrics that we would love to use but are 'too loud' to wear; this way you get to use those awesome fabrics and at the same time make your skirt unique.

I love the way this quick and simple lined patch pocket looks like a yoke pocket, because of the positioning and shape... but you don't need to adjust your skirt front pattern to achieve this.

Bobbie NOTHING COMES BETWEEN ME AND MY JEANS

No skirt collection is complete without a denim skirt! For this skirt recipe
I have chosen classic jeans features like the fly zip, a back yoke and orange
topstitching for my seam finishes. Timeless and dependable – this is a
classic staple.

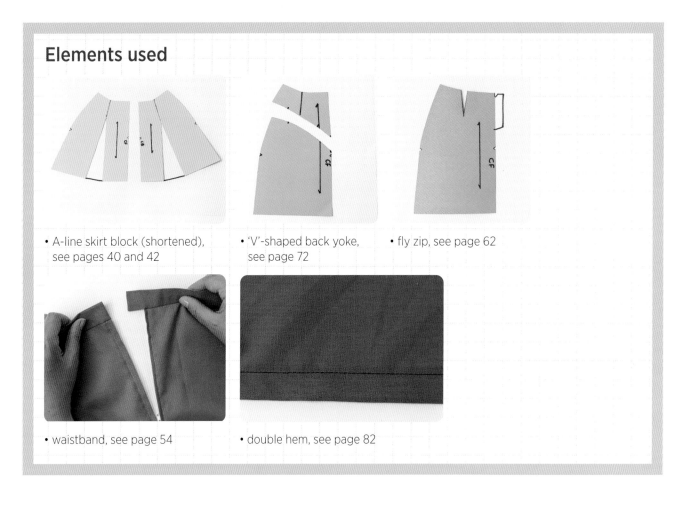

Elements used

- A-line skirt block (shortened), see pages 40 and 42
- 'V'-shaped back yoke, see page 72
- fly zip, see page 62
- waistband, see page 54
- double hem, see page 82

Creating your pattern

1 Firstly, shorten your basic skirt block to your preferred length (see page 40), before adjusting your block to create an A-line skirt shape (see page 42). Remember to adjust both front and back pattern pieces.

2 Taking the back-skirt pattern only, draw out your yoke shape (see page 72); you will not need to close the dart as you have already done that when creating the A-line shape. I used a 'V'-shaped yoke, as shown on page 107. Remember to make notches along the yoke line before cutting out – these will help you to join the pieces back together later on.

3 Taking the front pattern piece, add your zip allowance to the top of the centre front. Make sure to mark out where the zip teeth end and also the centre front of the skirt. You will also need to create a pattern for your zip guard – this needs to be a little longer than the zip length and about 12cm (4¾in) wide (see page 62).

4 To draft my waistband length, I used my toile's waistline measurement plus 6cm (2½in) to give me extra for the zip guard that my waistband will need to cover. My finished waistband was 3cm (1¼in) wide.

5 Transfer all notches and grainline details to the paper pattern as well as your 1.5cm (⅝in) seam allowances. Note that none of the pattern pieces are to be placed on the fold, so seam allowances will be required on all edges of the patterns. Also, as you are double hemming your skirt, I would suggest adding 4cm (1½in) in total to the hemline (see page 82). Cut out your pattern pieces.

6 Position your patterns on your fabric. Pin in place, cut out and transfer the notches onto the fabric. Remember that the length of the waistband needs to follow the grainline of the fabric.

Making your skirt

1 For this skirt, I would suggest using a welt or flat-fell seam, coupled with a contrast topstitching where possible, to finish the seams and to add that 'denim' style detail (see page 21).

2 Start by joining the skirt front pieces, right sides together and insert the fly zip (see page 62). To complete the zip, use a contrast topstitching thread to sew the guard in place and for finishing the centre-front seam.

3 Attach the back yokes to the remaining back skirt pieces. Place them right sides together, matching the notches, then stitch in place (see page 73). Next, join the centre-back seams, right sides together, matching the yoke seams. Complete with topstitching detail.

4 Pin and stitch the skirt front to the skirt back with the right sides together at the side seams.

5 Interface your waistband piece, before pinning and stitching to the waistline of the skirt. Be mindful of the seam allowances here as you want a clean finish, and not an extra tab of fabric at either end of the waistband (see pages 54–55). To finish the waistband I topstitched around the edges with contrast thread.

6 For the finishing touch, press and double hem your skirt, topstitching with the contrast thread (see page 82). Now you can be forever in blue jeans!

It's all about the contrast topstitching for this skirt.

To help reduce bulk, I've used a cotton fabric for the zip guard rather than the denim.

The yoke and back seam is a place to really show off that contrast topstitching.

Kate STASH BUSTING WITH FLARE

This fabulous flared, 1970s-style, mid-length skirt utilizes a beautiful scrap piece of African printed fabric as a peekaboo detail. By adding details like the yoked pocket with flaps, lined waistband and bound hem, I was able to incorporate a special piece of fabric into the make, and do a little stash busting too!

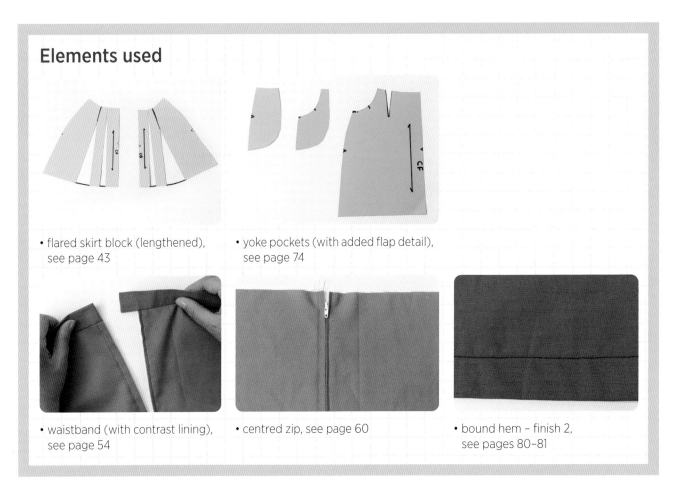

Elements used

- flared skirt block (lengthened), see page 43

- yoke pockets (with added flap detail), see page 74

- waistband (with contrast lining), see page 54

- centred zip, see page 60

- bound hem – finish 2, see pages 80–81

Creating your pattern

1 Firstly, lengthen your basic skirt block to your preferred length (see page 40), before adjusting your block to create a flared skirt shape (see page 43). Remember to adjust both front and back pattern pieces.

2 Taking the front skirt pattern only, begin to draft your yoke pocket (see page 74) remembering to add notches and grainlines to your pattern pieces to help you line up the fabric pieces later. You will end up with three pattern pieces: the skirt front with a pocket opening shape cut out, the pocket yoke, which will need to be in the main fabric, and the pocket lining, which I cut from a contrast fabric.

3 For my design, I added an extra 'flap' to the pocket. This is purely for detail rather than function. It is a simple triangle shape, inserted between the pocket opening and pocket lining, so one edge will need to be the same shape as the pocket opening. If you are going to add this detail too, you will need to cut out the pattern twice for each pocket, as you need a right and wrong side to give you an enclosed seam and a clean edge.

4 Draw out your waistband length using your natural waist measurement plus 15cm (6in) for a speedy draft (see page 54). You will not need to double the width of your waistband fabric this time; instead, cut your intended width (plus seam allowances) from both your main and lining fabrics. These pattern pieces will be sewn back together, to create the band, rather than using a single folded fabric piece.

5 Transfer all notches and grainline details to the paper pattern as well as your 1.5cm (⅝in) seam allowances. Note that the front skirt piece will be placed on the fold, so no seam allowances will need to be added here. Also, as you are binding your hem, add 1.5cm (⅝in) at the hemline (see page 80). Cut out your patterns.

6 Position your skirt front, skirt back, pocket yoke, flap outer and waistband patterns onto the main fabric. Position your waistband lining, pocket lining and flap lining patterns onto contrast fabric (your bias binding will also be cut from contrast fabric). Pin in place, cut out and transfer all notches onto the fabric. Remember that the length of the waistband needs to follow the grainline of the fabric.

Making your skirt

1 If you are adding the pocket flaps, make these first: place a lining piece with a main fabric piece right sides together, then stitch, clip and turn out before pressing and finishing with a topstitch. Repeat, so you have one for each side.

2 Construct the yoke pockets. Start by adding interfacing to the pocket openings on the skirt front (see page 75). Remember to add the 'flap' in between the skirt front and pocket lining before pinning together and completing the pockets as usual (see pages 75–76).

3 Prepare your two back skirt pieces for inserting your zip, making sure all notches line up first (see page 60).

4 Bring the front and back skirt pieces together at the side seams. Matching all notches, pin and stitch in place before pressing and finishing the seams.

5 Interface your waistband piece, then sew the outer and lining pieces together, right sides facing. Open out this piece, press the seam open and press under the lining seam allowance, before attaching the waistband to your skirt's waistline (see page 55). To finish the waistband, hand-stitch the lining to the skirt.

6 Finish the skirt with a bound hem (see finish 2 on page 81). You'll be running up that hill in no time!

Don't be afraid to add little features to your skirt like this shaped tab...

... or this contrast facing.

Use a contrasting thread for a sprinkle of topstitching detail.

Add a contrast pocket flap to create a unique feature.

Joni A-LINE... WITH A TWIST!

I fell in love with this fabric as soon as I saw it and wanted to play around with the strong striped tapestry detail. By placing the pattern on the bias and adding a centre-front seam, the fabric's striped detail creates an eye-catching chevron. Pockets are always a must, but rather than making them a visible feature that would interfere with the fabric pattern, I chose inseam pockets instead.

Elements used

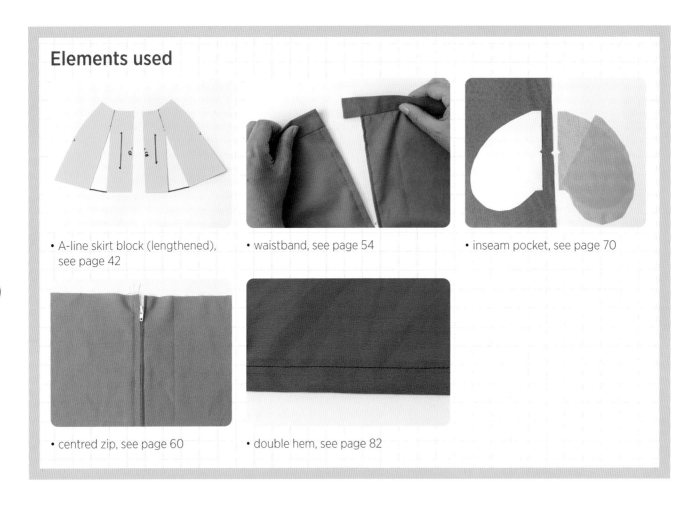

- A-line skirt block (lengthened), see page 42

- waistband, see page 54

- inseam pocket, see page 70

- centred zip, see page 60

- double hem, see page 82

Creating your pattern

1 Adjust your basic skirt block to create an A-line skirt shape (see page 42) then extend the length as you wish (see page 40). Remember to adjust both the front and back pattern pieces before tracing them onto drafting paper.

2 On fabric, draw out your waistband using your natural waist measurement plus 15cm (6in) for speed (see page 54) – remember that the length of the waistband needs to follow the grainline of the fabric.

3 Draw out your inseam pocket shape on paper – I like to draw around my hand for a quick pattern template (see page 70). When it comes to cutting out you are going to need a set of two pockets – meaning you will need to cut the pocket piece out twice but make sure you flip the pattern for one of them.

4 Add your 1.5cm (⅝in) seam allowances and transfer all notches and grainline details to the paper patterns. Note that your front and back skirt patterns BOTH need to have two separate pattern pieces in order to create the centre-front and centre-back seams, therefore add seam allowances as they will not be placed on the fold. To create the chevron effect with a striped fabric you will need to redraw your pattern's grainline at 45 degrees. As well as creating a visual effect with the fabric, it will also add more swish to your skirt, as your paper pattern will be positioned at an angle on the fabric and cut on the bias (see page 20). As this skirt has a double hem, I would suggest adding 3cm (1¼in) to the hemline for this shape of skirt (see page 82). Cut out your patterns.

5 Position all the patterns onto fabric by lining up the new grainlines with the fabric's grainline. Pin in place, cut out and transfer the notches onto the fabric.

> ## Top tip
>
> When trying to pattern match, I find it easier to cut out my pattern pieces one at a time rather than when the fabric is folded, meaning you cut two pieces out at once. By cutting your skirt pattern pieces out on a single piece of fabric, you can make sure the fabric's pattern is meeting at the same points along the joining seams.

114

Making your skirt

1 Firstly, prepare your skirt front pieces: place them right sides together, making sure all the notches are lined up, pin, then sew together. Be careful not to over-stretch the seam, as the bias-cut pieces will move and stretch more than usual.

2 Next, take your back skirt pieces and follow the centred zip instructions on how to insert the zip (see page 60) into the centre-back seam.

3 Now move on to creating your inseam pockets – remember to keep your pocket pieces in pairs, so that they match up during construction. Once the pocket linings are attached, bring the front and back skirt pieces together, right sides facing. Stitch the side seams and pockets in place (see page 70), then press and finish the seams (see page 21).

4 To give your skirt's waistline a clean finish, it is now time to add the waistband. Interface your waistband fabric, then attach the waistband to the skirt by placing the right sides together. Match up the seams and notches by pinning and then stitching in place (see pages 54–55).

5 Finish off your skirt with a double hem (see page 82). Now it's time to give it a twirl!

By cutting the skirt's front and back patterns on the bias, I have created this chevron effect along the centre front and back seams (see below left and right). It was really important to take my time when cutting out my pattern pieces to ensure the fabric pattern matched when stitched together.

I couldn't resist adding pockets to this skirt, but rather than making them a visible feature that would interfere with the patterned detail, I chose inseam pockets instead.

Judy POCKETS FULL OF GATHERED DREAMS

This is my take on the classic gathered skirt with pockets. The abstract checked fabric inspired the idea, while I was on my fabric hunt for the book. Simple in design and practical with those patch pockets, this skirt can be easily dressed up or down, whether at home or away on your adventures.

Elements used

- gathered skirt block (lengthened), see page 49
- button placket, see page 64
- waistband, see page 54
- unlined patch pockets, see page 69
- double hem, see page 82

Creating your pattern

1 Firstly, adjust the length of your basic skirt block to give you a mid-length skirt (see page 40). Remember to adjust both front and back pattern pieces.

2 Next, adjust your pattern to create a gathered skirt at the waistline (see page 49). If you want to add more volume to the hemline of the skirt, like I have, separate the pattern sections at both the waist and hemlines. Otherwise, pivot the sections at the hem to get a more tulip-shaped skirt.

3 Draw out your button placket pattern (see page 64). You only need to draft this once, but remember to cut out twice so you have a placket for the left- and right-hand sides of the skirt.

4 To create my waistband, I used my natural waist measurement plus 6cm (2½in) to account for the button placket. My finished waistband was 2.5cm (1in) wide. Remember when cutting out that the length of the waistband needs to follow the grainline of the fabric (see page 54).

5 When making your patch pockets, I would recommend creating a pattern. The shape is your choice, but use the same pattern for both pockets. Mark out where you want your pockets on the front skirt pattern, to ensure they are symmetrical when it comes to stitching it all together (see page 69).

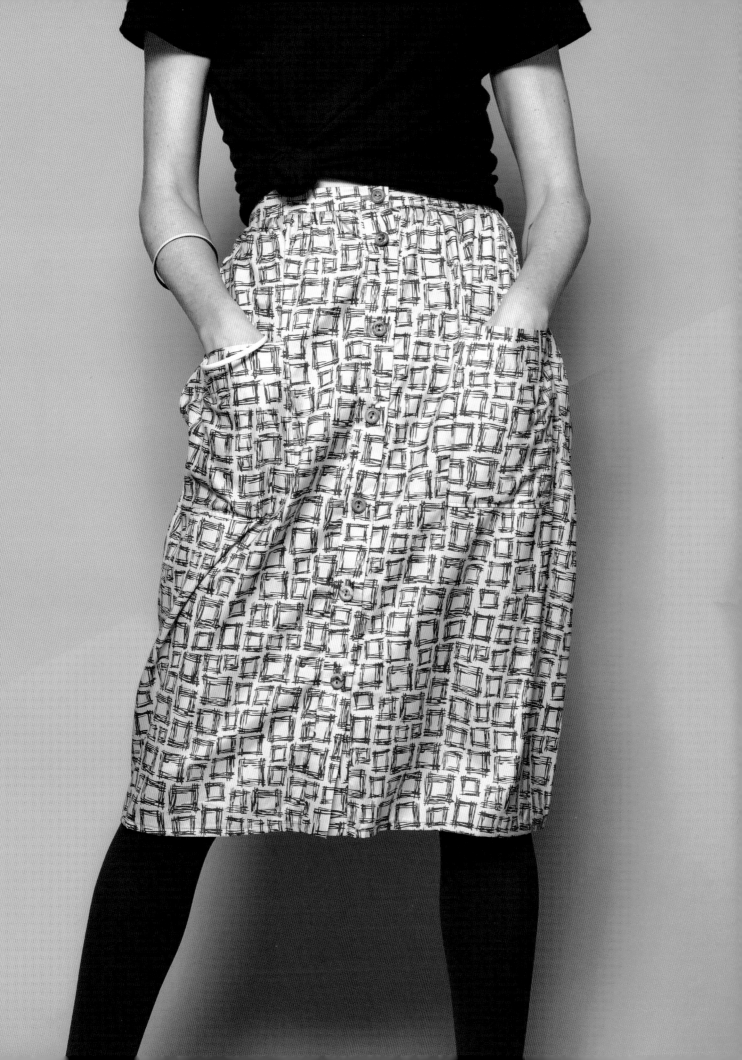

6 Transfer all notches and grainline details to the paper pattern as well as your 1.5cm (⅝in) seam allowances. Note that the back-skirt pattern is to be placed on the fold, and you are adding a placket, so you do not need to add seam allowances at the centre-back or centre-front. As you are double hemming your skirt, I would suggest adding 3cm (1¼in) in total to the hemline for this shape of skirt. Cut out your patterns.

7 Position the patterns onto your fabric, with the back-skirt pattern on the fold. Pin in place, cut out and transfer the notches to the fabric.

Making your skirt

1 Begin by making your unlined patched pockets (see page 69) so they can be attached to the skirt fronts at the marked positions. I find attaching the patch pockets before joining the skirt pieces together easier, as you are dealing with a flat piece of fabric rather than a circular skirt.

2 Prepare your button plackets by interfacing and pressing the seam allowances under, so they can be stitched to the centre fronts of both front skirt pieces, remembering to stop sewing where your finished hemline will end (see page 64). Be mindful that even though your plackets are the same shape, one is for the right, and one the left, so they will need to be interfaced and attached accordingly.

3 With the right sides facing, pin and stitch the front and back skirt pieces together, making sure all seams and notches match. Finish the seams.

4 Interface your waistband piece (see page 54), before gathering your skirt's waistline (see page 51) ready to insert into the waistband. Make sure the top of the plackets are folded and seams are enclosed before stitching in place. Be mindful of the seam allowances here as well, as you want a clean finish, not an extra tab of fabric (see page 54).

5 Double hem your skirt, so that you can finish off your button placket (see pages 82 and 64) and enclose all the raw edges. To finish, mark out and stitch your buttonholes and buttons onto the placket and waistband. Now go fill those pockets full of sewing dreams!

Sometimes a fabric dictates the design of a garment – for me, this abstract check just had to be made into a gathered skirt with patch pockets....

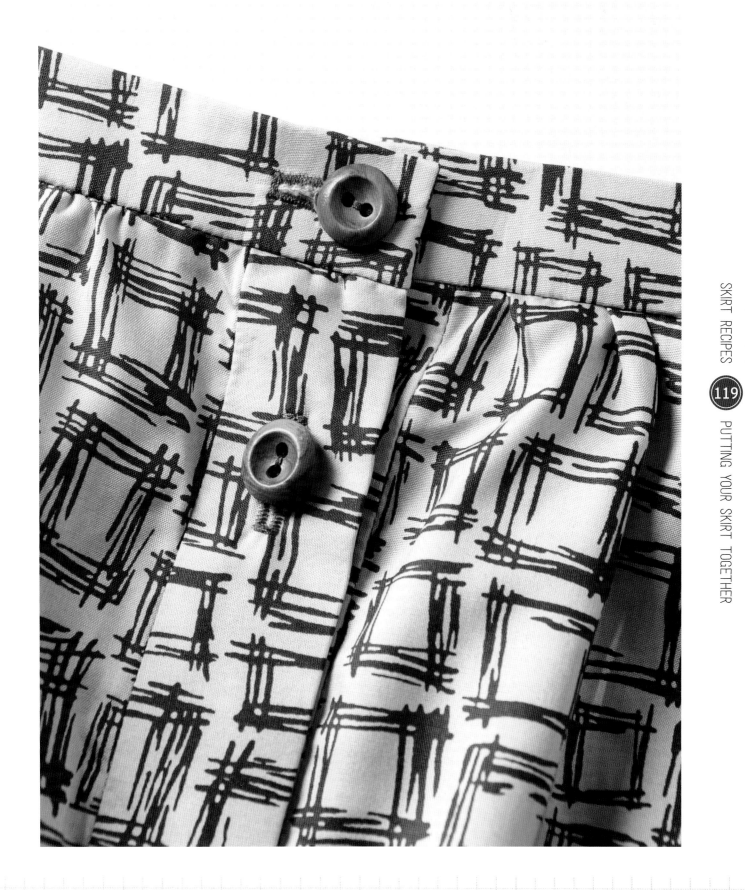

... and a front button placket finished with buttonholes and wooden buttons.

Jasmine SUMMER BREEZE: A TIERED DELIGHT

For this skirt recipe, the fabric influenced the design. The floral print and drape of the material instantly made me think of summer evenings and being on holiday. It gives a figure-hugging fit around the hips and waist, then the gathered tiers allow you to swish as you walk bare-footed in the sand.

Elements used

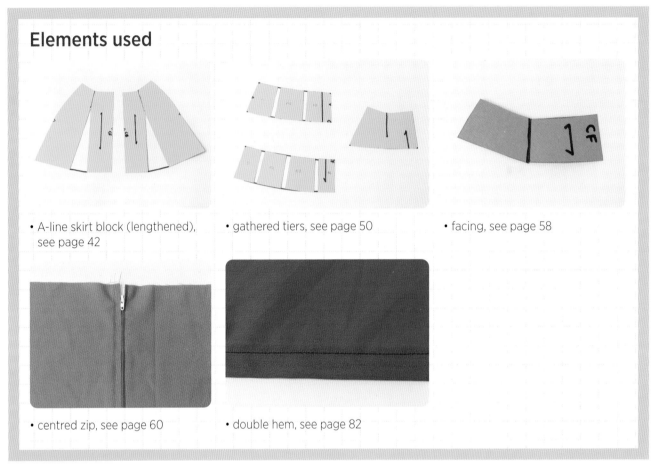

- A-line skirt block (lengthened), see page 42

- gathered tiers, see page 50

- facing, see page 58

- centred zip, see page 60

- double hem, see page 82

Creating your pattern

1 This skirt requires several changes to your block – so take your time with it. Extend the length of your basic skirt block to your chosen length (see page 40), before creating an A-line skirt shape (see page 42). Remember to adjust both front and back pattern pieces before tracing onto drafting paper.

2 Section off your skirt pattern to create the tiers – I have chosen three tiers, but you can add more if you wish (see page 50). Splice the second and third tier into sections, so that you can evenly distribute the extra width required to make the gathers. Remember that with each tier you will need to increase the width added every time, to create the gathers.

3 Create your facing pattern by using the first 5cm (2in) of your pattern front and back pieces (see page 58) – note that you will not need to close the dart positions as you already did this when creating the A-line shape in step 1.

4 Add 1.5cm (⅝in) seam allowances – as all front pattern pieces will be placed on the fold, no seam allowances will be required along the centre-front positions. As you are double hemming your skirt, I would suggest adding 3cm (1¼in) in total to the hemline for this shape of skirt (see page 82). Ensure that all grainlines and notches are transferred to all paper patterns before cutting out, especially the centre-front and centre-back positions, as this will help you to evenly distribute the gathers later on.

5 Position all the patterns onto fabric; pin in place, cut out and transfer the notches onto the fabric.

Making your skirt

1 Prepare your front skirt and back skirt pieces for gathering (see page 51) before matching the notches, pinning and then stitching the tiers together. Finish the seam edges as you want (see page 21) and then press them towards the waistline.

2 With the right sides together, join your centre-back seam, matching the tiered seams in preparation for your centred zip insertion. Insert the zip (see page 60).

3 Bring the front and back skirt pieces together with the right sides together. Ensure all tiered seams are matching before stitching the side seams together, press and finish the seams (see page 21).

4 It's now time to add the facing. Interface your facing pieces before sewing the side seams together. Add your facing to the waistline of your skirt by placing the right sides together, matching up the seams and notches, then pin and stitch in place (see page 58).

5 Complete your skirt by finishing off with a double hem (see page 82). Now it's time for that walk along the beach!

The centred zip and faced waistline edge give you a clean, crisp finish.

I love the way the gathers add volume to the
skirt as each tier is added.

Grace BOX-WRAPPED BEAUTY

When thinking about this design, I knew I wanted to create something a bit special with drama and glamour, while keeping it simple enough to be able to make at speed. I decided on a wrap skirt with box pleats in the front and back and an oversized wrapped waistband to create the dramatic draped bow... perfect for a last-minute make for special occasions.

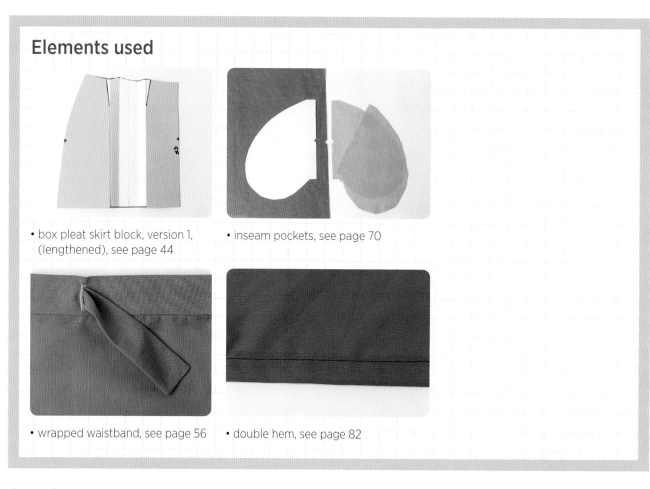

Elements used

- box pleat skirt block, version 1, (lengthened), see page 44
- inseam pockets, see page 70
- wrapped waistband, see page 56
- double hem, see page 82

Creating your pattern

1 Adjust the length of your basic skirt block to give you a full-length skirt (see page 40); remember that you will need to adjust both the front and back pattern pieces. To add the box pleat allowances, you will also need to adjust your pattern at the dart positions in the back and front pieces (see page 44). Trace your patterns onto drafting paper: you will need one box-pleated back section, one box-pleated front, and one regular, unbox-pleated front, to complete the wrap.

2 Draw out your inseam pocket shape on paper – I like to draw around my hand for a quick pattern template (see page 70). When it comes to cutting out, you are going to need a set of two pockets – meaning you will need to cut the pocket piece out twice but make sure you flip the pattern for one of them.

3 To create your wrapped waistband you will be using your natural waist measurement and adding extra length for the wrap and bow. The calculations on page 56 give you a modest bow but I have added about 1.5m (1½yd) to my waist measurement; how large you create your bow is totally up to you. Whatever the length, remember to be mindful of the grain of the fabric when it comes to cutting out. You may need to join fabric together to obtain the right length. My finished waistband was 2.5cm (1in) wide.

4 Transfer all notches and grainline details onto the paper pattern along with your 1.5cm (⅝in) seam allowance to all edges apart from the hemline. Note that all your pattern pieces are to be placed on the fold, along the centre-front and centre-back positions, so no seam allowance will be needed here. I would suggest adding 4cm (1½in) in total for the double hem finish for this skirt. Cut out your pieces.

5 Position your patterns onto your fabric. Pin in place, cut out and transfer all your notches to the fabric.

Making your skirt

1 Sew up the darts in the unbox-pleated front skirt piece.

2 Create the box pleats in your remaining front and back skirt pieces (see page 45), making sure all notches line up. Pin and stitch the pleats in place.

3 Next you will create your inseam pockets. Keep your pocket pieces in pairs, so that they match up during construction. As this is a wrap skirt, you need to be mindful that you attach the right pocket to the right-hand seam of the front skirt with the box pleats; you add the left pocket to the left-hand seam of the front skirt with darts (see page 70). For the back skirt piece, add the pockets as normal. Once the pockets are attached, bring the front and back skirt pieces together with the right sides and pockets together. Stitch the side seams and pockets in place. Press and finish the seam edges.

4 Before adding your wrapped waistband, double hem the remaining side seams of your two front skirt pieces, to give you a clean edge to insert into the waistband.

5 If need be, join your waistband pieces together to create one long piece. Interface your waistband, but only the section that will attach to the waistline of the skirt. Attach your waistband to the waistline of your skirt by placing them right sides together, then stitch in place (see page 56); finish the waistband by adding a buttonhole to pass the band through and then stitch the raw edge of the waistband closed.

6 Double hem your skirt hem to finish (see page 82), then sip that cocktail to celebrate!

To create the oversized bow, simply add more length to your wrapped waistband.

Because who doesn't love a pocket – especially in a formal garment!

The box pleats in the front and the back of this wrapped
skirt add movement, volume and detail.